T0103919

WALKING THE PATHWAY OF LIFE

MERRILL PHILLIPS

Trafford rev. 03/14/2014

 www.trafford.com

North America & international
toll-free: 1 888 232 4444 (USA & Canada)
fax: 812 355 4082

TO LOVE SOMEONE ENOUGH

TO LET THEM GO DESCRIBES

THE KIND OF LOVE GOD HAS

FOR US.

MERRILL PHILLIPS

CONTENTS

IS THERE A GOD

Jeremiah 31:33
But this is the covenant that I will make with the house of Israel after those days, says the Lord; I will put My law in their minds, and write it in their hearts; and I will be their God and they shall be My people.

How someone can make the statement that there is no God I understand not. What other explanation can there be for this world and universe that we live in, surly it did not just happen by random chance.

I personally have had too many encounters with our Lord and Savior (Jesus Christ) to say that there is no evidence of a being (God) capable of creating all that we observe.

Without God, I would have long ago left this world due to my behavior and lifestyle that I have lived in the past.

I am by no means proud of all that I have done and have only one explanation as to why I am still living (God) and at this time fulfilling my calling as a writer of which I was not trained to do nor was I qualified to write.

When I first answered my calling to write I had no idea of how to go about it or what to say. While in high school, English was my worse subject and I had no interest whatsoever in becoming a writer.

The first article that I wrote was poorly written and some of my articles now are still poorly written, but that first article did have a central theme that was based on a personal experience with the addition of alcohol.

As time passed my knowledge about writing improved, the more I wrote the better I became and my confidence grew that I could fulfill that which God had called me to do.

Over the years, I have come to realize that when God calls someone to fulfill that which He wants them to do that He will give them the knowledge that they need to fulfill their calling.

I have also come to realize that if I had of chosen to ignore my calling that one-day I would have to stand before God and explain why I did not do as He asked and to me that would be a very scary situation to be in.

Through writing, I have grown spiritually and have come to trust God for my every need and I know that one day that which I have written will be used for the advancement of His kingdom here on earth.

That to me is reason enough to keep on writing and not worry about how I will support myself in the process.

God has done so many amazing things in my life that in no way can I or could I ever deny that there is a God who loves us all enough to sacrifice His only Son so that we can have a way to be free of sin.

We will always be tempted by sin, but God has provided a way so that we can avoid being overwhelmed or lost because of sin.

God not only created all that we observe, but He is in complete control of all that goes on in this world.

Why God allows some things to happen I know not, but I do know that when all is said and done those who trust and believe in Jesus Christ shall endure and live in His presence for eternity.

To me that is what this life is all about, learning to trust and believe in God and preparing ourselves for that new life to come, which lies beyond the grave.

I am convinced that life beyond the grave exists. That it is ours to have if we want it and that the only way to achieve it is to believe that Jesus Christ is who He claims to be. The one and only Son of God and that He died for our sins so that we might have life everlasting.

GIFTS

2 Timothy 1:6
Therefore I remind you to stir up the gift of God which
is in you through the laying on of my hands.

There isn't anything any more fulfilling or meaningful than to be given a gift from God.

Whether it is in the middle of the night or during the day God speaks to those who He chooses to work for Him.

It is up to each one who is called to either accept their calling or to refuse it, God will not force anything upon anyone.

No matter what the calling is, God will supply everything that is needed to carry out that calling.

God calls not those with a prideful heart, but the lowly in heart and those who are willing to step forth and be a part in His plan for mankind.

Not all are called, for all are not willing to give up earthly treasures and pleasures to do something that they may never be compensated for in this life.

The laying up of treasures in heaven seem foreign to most, for they want their reward here and now, so that they can enjoy it while still here on earth.

Those who God calls still have to be careful so as not to allow any good fortune that might come their way to interfere with what they were called to do.

So very often, the called of God struggle with life and do not receive great compensation for their efforts.

They fulfill their calling with humbleness of heart and expect nothing but the pleasure of serving God as their compensation.

To refuse to fulfill one's calling is to miss out on the greatest opportunity to serve God that they will ever have.

God knows the heart of those whom He calls and knows beforehand that they are capable of doing what He puts on their heart to do and what they don't know He will supply them as they obey.

This is indeed the case with me, for I have no so called formal education, nor did I think myself capable of writing as God has called me to do.

At first, I struggled and knew not what to write, but as time went on and I allowed the Holy Spirit to guide me, more and more it became clear that I was capable of doing what I was asked to do.

I slowly lost the fear that I might offend someone or that they might not like what I had to say, but when you are doing, God's will in your life it matters not what others might think or say.

Whether my offerings are made available to the public in my lifetime is not for me to worry about, I do know however that the day will come when they will be used in ways that I now do not know.

My main concern is to see to it that I keep on writing until God calls me home and then I will know if I fulfilled my calling to His satisfaction.

From the human standpoint it would be nice to enjoy the fruits of my labor while still here on earth. That is not likely to happen so I am satisfied to know that God loved me enough to grant me the privilege of working for Him and helping my fellowman understand the great love that God has for all of us.

I know of no greater calling than to be called by God to something that I have come to love and want to spend my last days doing and I know that God will leave me here long enough to finish what He has laid on my heart to do.

I know that my offerings may not compare to the great poets and authors that have gone before me, but I do rejoice in the fact that God did call me to write and that in itself is the greatest thing that has ever happened to a poor country boy like myself.

God is supreme and God makes no mistakes and to this end I bow my head and bend my knees before His Holy throne and subject myself to His will and thank Him from the bottom of my heart for calling upon me to work for Him.

To work in silence without expectation of monetary compensation may seem foolish to most, but to me I have already been compensated by being asked to write for God. What more could anyone want than that?

God has and will continue to supply all of my needs and I need nothing more than this out of life. I envy not those with great wealth, for I believe that I have received a gift that cannot be bought with all of the wealth in the world. Worldly wealth is but for a short while, Godly wealth is for eternity.

I mean not to sound like I think myself better than anyone else, for I know that I am but a lowly sinner trying to endure the trials of this life and do that which will enable me to spend eternity with our creator, God.

JUST A NOTE OF THANKS

Psalm 100:4
Enter into His gates with thanksgiving, and into His courts with praise. Be thankful to Him, and bless His name.

O Lamb of God, I come before Thee with an open and contrite heart.

I come with the expectation of receiving a blessing of love and guidance.

I come to give Thee thanks for opening the door that leads to Thy throne.

I give thanks for your guidance in writing what You want me to convey and for providing an outlet where these writings might be a benefit to others.

I pray that through these writings others might find some answers to their problems and comfort in their times of need.

Through writing, I have grown in Thy ways and have come to have a greater understanding of You, O God, and what You want for all of us.

I have come to realize that You want all of mankind to accept Your Son, Jesus Christ, as Lord and Master of their lives, so that when we leave this world we will be able to spend eternity with You.

May my humble offerings be used wisely and to the benefit of those who seek to change, and that they might lead to a turning point in the lives of many.

Just as You have touched my life with Your mighty healing hand, may others receive a similar healing experience, and come to know You as I have.

Whether I live a short life or a long life, I will continue to do my best to fulfill what You have called me to do.

I give unto You, almighty God, the praise and honor that is due You, now and forevermore.

I BELIEVE

Hebrews 11:6
But without faith it is impossible to please Him, for he who comes to God must believe that He is, and that He is a rewarder of those who diligently seek Him.

I believe in Jesus Christ as the Son of God who came to be a sacrificial lamb for the sins of man.

He came to free those who believe and release them from the bondage of sin.

Freed us so that after we pass through the door of death we can live with God as Jesus lived with us, a sin free life.

As we live now we are not capable of seeing through that cloud of sin and seeing man as one day he will be.

The pleasures of the flesh (more commonly known as sin) is what forms that cloud of sin.

Jesus was the only sinless one to ever live on earth, as the Son of God He opened the door to a sinless life for us.

When Jesus died on the cross at Calvary, He left us a comforter who we know as the Holy Ghost or Holy Spirit, whichever you prefer.

Through the Holy Ghost, we have a direct channel to God and God through the Holy Ghost communicates with us and passes on the gifts that God bestows upon His chosen.

These gifts are for the promotion of God's kingdom here on earth, and by exercising our God given gifts, we are able to help our fellowman through his trials of life.

This also enables us to fulfill Galatians 6:2. "Bear one another's burdens, and thus fulfill the law of Christ."

As there is heaven for all believers, so is there a hell for those who refuse to believe that Jesus Christ is who He claims to be.

Upon passing from this life, we are appointed to reside either in heaven or in hell, according as to how we lived our life while here on earth.

Those who refuse to believe shall be cast into the lake of fire that burns with brimstone separated from God for eternity, those who believe shall dwell with God forever.

I believe in Jesus Christ as the Son of God, who came to earth to guide us on our journey through this life and that through Him I shall dwell with God forever.

Thus is the destiny of man.

I NEVER KNEW

Psalm 46:10
Be still and know that I am God; I will be exalted
among the nations, I will be exalted in the earth!

I never knew that I was lost; even though I believed in Jesus
and accepted God.

During my youth mother saw to it that I went to Sunday
school and taught me right from wrong.

In my teen years, I occasionally went to church and heard His
word, but I never really knew God.

To me God was God, but God had no special place in my life
or thinking, church or Sunday school was just a place to go on
Sunday mornings.

During these years, I made decisions and pretty much lived life
my way, I didn't know Jesus as my Savior or as the Son of God.

Just before going off to war I was baptized and went through
the act of believing, mostly to please my mother.

I just went along with the flow of life and worked hard and
when I thought about Jesus it was what He could do for me, not
what I could do for Him.

Occasionally I helped my neighbors and felt good about it and
thought that I was doing the work of the Lord.

In reality I was running towards hell as fast as my legs would
carry me and did not even know it, I was a good guy and helped
someone whenever I could. What else was I supposed to do?

I was blind and did not want to see, If I had died during this
period in my life I would have been cast into outer darkness,
tormented for eternity.

Even though I had good intentions I was living life my way
with no thought of where I would spend eternity.

There are many ways to deceive ourselves and think that we are doing the work of the Lord, but until we ask God to come into our lives and take Him seriously, we are just a walking time bomb headed for self-destruction.

Once we decide to accept God into our lives we have to come to grips with ourselves and learn among other things, self-discipline to where we not only control our actions, but also our thoughts.

At first attempts, it may seem to be an impossible task, but the more we allow God, Jesus Christ, and the Holy Spirit to have an influence in our lives we begin to triumph over the temptations of the secular world.

Left alone, no matter how good we think ourselves to be, self will destroy itself, but under the influence of God self will flourish.

In reality this world and the life we have is but a training exercise for us to come to know God and to come to grips as to where we want to spend eternity.

The more we seek God and Jesus Christ as the Son of God the closer we come to God, Jesus, and the Holy Ghost, and allow them to have control of our lives and ask "What can I do for you Lord while I am here?", rather than what they can do for us.

Once started on the road to eternity with our Creator, hold fast, look not back, but rather keep your eyes on the final goal of what this life is all about, spending eternity with our triune God.

EVER ONWARD

Matthew 6:251
Therefore I say to you, do not worry about your life, what you will eat or what you will drink; nor about your body, what you will put on. Is not life more than food and the body more than clothing?

Ever onward we climb the ladder of life, sometimes stumbling, picking ourselves up we start again.

Never giving up as we traverse the obstacles of life, ever onward through the pains of life we climb.

Arthur (arthritis) creeps into our joints and slows us a bit, but ever onward we climb the ladder of life.

For some the life giving juices of the body begin to slow, the Dr. says, "I must cut you and bypass those plugged arteries and then onward you can go."

After a few months of rest, you feel like new as you proudly display the railroad tracks up and down your chest.

Other friends (physical disabilities) try to join you on your road of life, and for the most part you say no, but occasionally one will hitch a ride and cause you to slide, but that's all right for that is the way of life.

Then comes Hyper (hypertension) and tries to slow us to a place where Rigor (Rigormortis) can set in, but keep moving my friend and perhaps he will pass you by, for a while at least.

By now you realize that your days are short and you put your affairs in order and await the great reaper. Then low and behold you get a new grasp on life and you stand tall and shout, "Not yet my friend, I can still see many rungs of the ladder of life yet before me. If you don't mind I think I will just stay around and keep on climbing the ladder of life and enjoy what God has for me."

The moral of the story is, "Never give up, always look forward to tomorrow, but live today as though it were going to be your last and God will bless you in many ways."

FEAR NOT

Romans 6:23
For the wages of sin is death, but the gift of God is eternal life in Jesus Christ our Lord.

Death is not to be feared, it is to be embraced without fear. Life here on earth is but a few short years.

Eternity is forever, a place of joy or a place of torment and pain. It is ours to choose while here on earth we remain.

God is waiting on the other side of death's door, waiting to welcome us home.

This body was created to decay and disappear from view; our soul was created to live forever.

Death comes to all, no one is left behind.

When we open our eyes through death, we will see the beauty of heaven if God so decrees and understand why we were born to live on earth.

All mysteries of life will become apparent and we will be free from the encumbrances of the body.

As death approaches fear it not, embrace it with the knowledge that Jesus Christ has prepared a place for us to abide in the new life to come.

IN BOLDNESS OF LOVE

1Corinthians 12:4-7

Love suffers long and is kind; love does not envy; love
does not parade itself, is not puffed; does not behave
rudely, does not seek its own, is not provoked, thinks
no evil; does not rejoice in iniquity, but rejoices in the
truth; bears all things, believes all things, hopes all
things, endures all things.

Approach God in the boldness of love, not in the timidity
of fear.

God is not to be feared, for He is a God of love and has
nothing but love to bestow on those who follow His ways.

There is no sin so egregious that God cannot forgive through
repentance.

It is we who have to change our way of thinking, in changing,
our heart will be open to the word of God and that in turn will
change our way of thinking and our lives.

God's love encompasses all and will surface through us as we
touch the lives of others for the good.

Physical fear of God keeps us from approaching God in the
attitude of repentance, we expect God to strike us down because of
the sin that we are engage in.

God is the same today as He was yesterday, and will be the
same tomorrow, it is we who sways in the wind, blowing one way
today and another way tomorrow.

Often we bend with the wind, in search of we know not what,
we hate to get out of our comfort zone.

We make our life harder than it needs to be, we complicate our
life by trying to live our life outside of God's influence and find
nothing but heartache for our trouble.

Many fear that if they give up self-control that they will lose all that they have or want out of life.

They worry and fear that God is not capable of helping them when and where they think He should.

Self-control and self-will has ruined many a good person, whereas if they had turned to God and submitted to His will their problems would disappear or dramatically improve for the better.

God wants nothing but the best for us and would provide it if only we would submit to His will, not our own.

There are two ways to fear God, one is through love and the other is through the fear of retribution, but God will never seek revenge, no, not even on the worst of sinners.

God has nothing but love for us, and even when He reprimands us He does it in love and will guide us if only we would allow Him to do so.

Be bold in love when approaching the throne of God, but always in humbleness of heart and always be willing to put self aside and allow God to have His way with you.

IN GOD'S HANDS

Acts 7:55
But he, being full of the Holy Spirit, gazed into heaven and saw the glory of God, and Jesus standing at the right hand of God.

Life here on earth may be a few short years with few tears or it may be many years with many trials and tribulations.

Whether short or long is not ours to determine, it is in God's hands and in His will as to how long we shall live.

It is however our responsibility to spend our years here on earth wisely, investing our time and effort in learning and teaching our children the way that God would have us live.

The closer to death we get the stronger our faith should be, for to leave this world without a clue as to where we will spend eternity is a disaster indeed.

Blindly following a false teacher can and will lead to falling into the great abyss.

Be independent and think for yourself and check out the doctrine of those whom you wish to be associated with.

Use the Bible as you base reference, for the Bible is the inspired word of God and should be our final board of arbitration in all disputes.

Use the Bible as your friend and guide and you will arrive in heaven when on this earth you no longer reside.

There are only two places where we can go when this world we leave, one is heaven and the other is hell.

If you think that there is hell here on earth, it pales in comparison to the real hell beyond the grave.

The same thing can be said about heaven, if you think heaven is here on earth, it too cannot compare to heaven beyond the grave and what it has to offer.

Heaven or hell is our choice to make, God would have no one to be lost, but the final decision is ours and ours alone.

IN HIS HANDS

Ephesians 2:8
For by grace you have been saved through faith, and
that not of yourselves; it is a gift of God.

I have come to understand that my whole life is in God's
hands, every breath that I take is by His grace.

Without God, I would have long ago been dead, dead in sin
and would have lost my place in his chain of command.

First there was Adam and Eve who are the only two people to
ever live in the Garden of Eden.

When they sinned and lost their place in the Garden of Eden,
it was incumbent upon God to cast man into darkness according
to His plan.

It was man, not God who disobeyed; it was man who deserved
to be cast into darkness for his sinful ways.

God had and has other plans for those who heed His voice and
walk the straight and narrow.

This pathway leads to a new tomorrow, a new beginning where
sin is trod underfoot.

A new tomorrow where the love of God prevails and rescues
man from the condemnation of sin.

A sin free environment where man will be treated as royalty
and will feed upon the true milk and honey.

From the sins of Adam and Eve to the glory of Paradise is a
long journey for mankind.

We are in a play that is being acted out on the stage of life with
but one thing in mind, the redemption of mankind.

Redeemed we will be if we follow Jesus Christ, for it is the will
of God that we all be renewed as we pass through the fires of life.

Burned and charred a little bit by the fires of life, but not beyond the redemptive love of God.

God sent his Son, Jesus Christ, as an atonement for our sins and through Him we can and shall be redeemed to our rightful place in the kingdom of God.

God has sent his Son Jesus Christ to take our place on the cross, now it is up to each one to accept Jesus' redemptive work or reject it.

God has kept his promises, now it is up to you and me to follow His lead.

Are you ready to be tried by fire and take your place by the Lord's side?

Or are you one of those who are blinded by sin and cannot see the shinning star of life, Jesus Christ?

We are in God's hands, if we choose to be. It is our choice as to whom we believe and follow, Satan or God.

IN THEE I FIND PEACE

Romans 5:1
Therefore, having been justified by faith, we have peace
with God through our Lord Jesus Christ.

I will come unto Thee O Lord whether my pockets are full or
empty and praise Thy holy name.

In the morning or the dark of night I will seek Thee, I will
come before Thy throne and seek Thy will.

Lord God you are the fulfillment of my soul, in Thee I find
peace.

I will no longer stray from Thy sheepfold. I will seek Thee in all
that I do. Peace *shall be mine all of my days, I will dwell with Thee
forever.*

It is with Thee that I long to be, my soul thirsteth to see Thee
face to face and hear Your comforting words.

I will seek the shelter of Thy wings when the storm winds blow,
just the thought frees my soul.

When this world I leave, I pray that I will find life anew
beyond the grave.

I thank Thee Lord my God for this life that You have given
unto me, I fear that I have not lived the life that You had in store
for me.

You have been gracious and taken me back even after all of the
sin I have displayed.

Through the storms of life, you have guided me and kept my
ship of life from wrecking on some foreign shore.

Gracious Lord you have been with me even when I was lost in
the fog of sin.

I heard Your voice calling and yet I knew not how to reply until the night that You turned on the "Light", the night that You set me apart from the rest of the world and freed me from sin.

For that night, I will always thank You, on bended knee I crawl before Thy throne and give myself to Thee, to use as You will.

For these blessings and many more, I can only say thank you for loving me enough to set me free from the bondage of sin.

JESUS

Romans 10:9
That if you will confess with your mouth the Lord Jesus and believe in your heart that God has raised Him from the dead, you will be saved.

It was Jesus who made the difference in my life.

It was Jesus who died so that you and I might live.

Live beyond this life, live with Him for eternity.

It was Jesus who trod the ancient world and spread his Father's word and became the head of the "Church".

He preached love for all, especially for you and me.

It was Jesus who faced Satan alone so that you and I would not have to.

It was Jesus who defeated Satan while on the cross and set us free.

All who believe that Jesus is the Son of God will never die.

When trouble comes, it is Jesus who we can go to and get help in overcoming our problems.

There is only one "Jesus", the door through which we must pass to get to heaven, yes, it is Jesus.

Jesus stands as a "Light" for the whole world to see, His "Light" will never fade or pass away, it will heal all who bathe in its glory.

From before the world was formed until it fades away Jesus will remain as He has always been, the Savior of all who follow His ways.

JESUS IS CALLLING

Jeremiah 33:3
Call to Me, and I will answer you, and show you great
and mighty things, which you do not know.

When Jesus called out "Lazarus, come forth," He was also
calling unto us of today.

He is calling us to come forth unto Him and disengage from
the sins of the world.

He is calling us to be born again, born of the spirit, to a new
life that will lead to eternal life with Him.

Jesus is trying to awaken us in our hearts to follow Him and
live as a Christian should.

Without malice in our hearts, with nothing but love towards
our fellowman.

He is asking us to forgive and return love for transgressions
against us.

Jesus is asking to be our Savior and live a life exemplifying his
love towards our fellowman.

That others may witness our desire to truly be a Christian in
every sense of the word.

"Lazarus, come forth," echoes across time and those who listen
hear it loud and clear.

This has been the changing point in many lives; times when
people take stock of their lives and make decisions as to how they
want to live and where they want to spend eternity.

Too many are deaf and do not hear Jesus calling, these are the
ones who face a very bleak future.

Deaf because they choose to be deaf and these same people
hesitate stepping forward as Lazarus did and allow Jesus to rule in
their lives.

It is unfortunate that many allow earthly treasures to be foremost in their lives, if they would only listen to the winds of time they would come to know that God holds nothing back from those who love Him, no, not even earthly goods.

Jesus is calling today, are you listening?

JESUS TOOK OUR PLACE

Luke 15:6-7
And when he comes home he will call together his friends and neighbors, saying to them, rejoice with me, for I have found my sheep which were lost. I say to you that likewise there will be more joy in heaven over one sinner who repents than over ninety-nine just persons who need no repentance.

Jesus came and took our place on the cross at Calvary and set us free.

Jesus took the sins of the world upon His shoulders so that we might live with Him in Paradise one day.

He gave His life for you and me when he died upon that cross at Calvary.

He was without sin and yet He became sin just for you and me.

The cross at Calvary is our door to heaven, through it, we will walk one day and be with the one who set us free.

The cross at Calvary is calling us while on this earth we trod so that we might be free from the sin that tries to bind us.

If it were not for Calvary we would still be blinded by sin and lose our way.

When sin tempts us, we will fear it not for Jesus paid the price when on that cross He hung that day at Calvary.

Take us home Lord Jesus, for this world is full of sin and we struggle every day so as not to be taken in and lose our place with Thee.

Thank you Lord Jesus for taking our place on the cross at Calvary and setting us free.

It is without a doubt the greatest thing that will ever happened to us, for free we will be when this life we leave and put on immortality.

Free indeed we will be because Jesus paid the price at Calvary when He suffered and died for you and me.

He did what no one else could do, He opened the door to heaven and set all of mankind free when upon that cross He died at Calvary.

JUST BELIEVE AND ASK

Luke 11:9-10
So I say to you, ask and it will be given to you; seek,
and you will find; knock and it will be opened to you.
For everyone who asks receives, and he who seeks finds,
and to him who knocks it will be opened.

Jesus is watching over us and if we acknowledge Him as the Son of God He will grant us eternal life, for He has the authority to do so.

If we acknowledge Him He will acknowledge us, if we will claim Him He will claim us before His Father, God, if we reject Him He will reject us.

It is just that simple; love and you will be loved ten times over.

Jesus is just waiting for us to allow Him to come into our hearts and He will do the rest.

We do not deserve His love because we are sinners, but He will forgive us our sins if we come to Him and confess and repent of our sins.

If we turn our lives over to Jesus, He will care for us and supply all of our needs.

Needs, not greed's, Jesus is not in the business of granting greed's, for the material things of this life are but for a short while, whereas the spiritual things are forever.

That is what Jesus wants to give us, He wants to give us eternal life, but He cannot do so unless we open the door, He stand without and knocks.

Jesus offers, we have to accept for ourselves, everyone on this planet has the same offer.

Many are lured by the riches of this world and follow false gods who have nothing to offer but the things of this world, all orchestrated by Satan.

We can gain much wealth, power, and the finest things of this world, but the only problem with this collection of wealth and power is that it cannot buy us even one second in heaven.

Only those who accept Jesus Christ on His terms and believe that He is who He claims to be will be allowed to enter the kingdom of God.

That is not to say that Christians cannot obtain wealth and power, because they can, they just do not let this wealth and power control their lives, they acknowledge that what they have as a gift from God is to be used in the advancement of His kingdom here on earth.

Shake off the lusts of this world, let God, Jesus Christ, and the Holy Spirit (triune God) be the center of your life and they will supply all of your needs and whatever else they know that you can handle without these things becoming a god in your life.

Foremost believe and then ask, ask not out of greed, but ask out of love and it shall be granted unto you.

JUST ONE DROP

Revelation 1:5-6
And from Jesus Christ, the faithful witness, the first
born from the dead, and the ruler over the kings of
the earth. To Him who loved us and washed us from
our sins in His own blood, and has made us kings and
priests to His God and Father, to Him be glory and
dominion forever and ever. Amen

Just one drop of our Lord's blood is enough to cleanse you
and me.

As He hung on that tree at Calvary His blood dropped one drip at
a time, it formed a river of forgiveness and salvation for all who believe.

I am fortunate enough to be one of those who has been
cleansed by the shed blood of the Lamb of God. Have you?

All who passed by that day as Jesus hung on that cross shook
their head at the only one who could wash them clean.

The Son of God could not and did not die that day; the cross
was His road back to heaven and His Father's side.

Even today some two thousand plus years after Jesus'
crucifixion just a single drop of our Savior's blood can still cleanse
all who stand before the cross of Calvary.

We, like Jesus one day shall rise from the grave and stand
before His throne to receive the blessings of his blood that He shed
at Calvary.

They thought that they had gotten rid of Jesus that day once
and for all, but Jesus still lives today, He hung on that tree as a
sacrifice for your sins and mine.

Bless all O Lord who seek to do Thy will, I ask that they be
cleansed as I was by just one drop of your blood that you shed
while hanging on that tree at Calvary.

LAST CHANCE

Revelation 7:13-14
Then one of the elders answered, saying to me, "Who are these arrayed in white robes, and where did they come from?" And I said to him, "Sir, you know." So he said to me, "These are the ones who came out of the great tribulation, and washed their robes and made them white in the blood of the Lamb."

The tribulation is an essential part of God's plan for mankind.

Many things will happen during this period of time, they are meant for the good of all who will go through the tribulation.

The Church of Christ will have been raptured and Satan will have his antichrist in power and all sorts of evil will prevail.

Among those who will be left behind after the rapture will be thousands who previously claimed to be Christians.

They may have proclaimed to be Christians, but in their hearts they never accepted Jesus as the Son of God.

They found all kinds of excuses to deny Jesus his rightful place in their lives.

Such as, "Tomorrow I will submit to Jesus' will, but today I have to make enough money to retire on."

Or they act as though they had given their lives to Jesus by going to church every Sunday and outwardly seem to believe Jesus' teachings, but in their hearts they never accepted Jesus for who He claims to be, the Son of God.

The excuses go on and on and none of them really has or had a personal relationship with Jesus Christ.

These are the ones who set in church right alongside of you and me and act out a lie when taking communion.

They have a false sense of adoration and a faith that is only skin deep, they run committees and are big church workers, and yet inwardly they do not trust what they cannot see or touch.

They might want to trust, but their faith is weak and their earthly possessions mean more to them than Jesus does.

They give of their time and money, but they do not give what God wants from all of us, total commitment.

The tribulation was designed by God to give all unbelievers one last chance to repent of their sins and come to Him with bowed head and a repentant heart.

The tribulation will be the last act of God to save His people before He releases his wrath upon the earth and destroy His creation with fire and brimstone.

Man has been warned beforehand to repent of his sins and accept Jesus Christ as the Son of God or else the wrath of God will come upon them.

Evil will climax during the seven years of tribulation and then with His mighty hand God will bring evil to an end and evil will never again exist.

On the other side the redemptive souls of the tribulation will join the "Church" of God and rejoice and sing praises before God's throne and spend eternity with Him.

The tribulation will be the last chance that man has to change his mind before being cast into the lake of fire, separated from God for eternity.

LAST JOURNEY

Numbers 6;24-26
The Lord bless and keep you; the Lord make His face
shine upon you and be gracious to you; the Lord lift up
His countenance upon you and give you peace.

O nce the spirit of man starts to leave, the body on its
journey to reunite with its creator nothing can stop or hinder it
from doing so.

This journey closes the chapter of life, as we know it for that
individual.

For those who are destined to reside in heaven after death there
is no sense of fear, just a quiet sense of peace prevails.

On the other hand, those destined to reside in hell die an
agonizing fearful death.

My own experience of my spirit leaving the body and
proceeding to its final destination was brief and never fully
completed.

I awoke before I fell prey to the final act of man here on earth,
the act of dying. It did however last long enough to let me know
that when my death does occur there will be no fear or anxiety
involved.

For this period of time I had the sensation of traveling through
time and space in a darkened surrounding, and yet the darkness
was not a complete darkness. There was as if streaks of dim light in
this darkness.

My experience convinced me that death is not to be feared
in any way. Any sense of my life here on earth was not present,
just a sense of complete peace and looking forward to what would
happen next.

Perhaps this experience was to confirm the fact that death really does not have any sting for those who are prepared for it through being a follower of Jesus Christ.

I resisted not the journey that I was on, nor did I have any sense of fear. I was on a journey to experience life after death and nothing could be any more real, except the real event.

I am convinced more than ever that those who choose not to follow Jesus Christ do indeed have much to fear and that they are on the road that leads to hell and all of its consequences.

Jesus really did take the sting out of death just as it is told in first Corinthians, chapter fifteen, verse fifty five. "O death, where is thy sting? O grave where is thy victory?"

Though at this time I did not complete my journey to eternal life I am convinced that when I do it will a journey that will hold no fear.

The Bible does hold the secrets of life, death and eternal life and for the followers of Jesus Christ there will be no fear when this earthly life ends.

For a brief moment, I had entered a path where there was complete obedience to God. Some might fight their trip to life beyond death because of their unbelief, but for the believer it is a long awaited journey to true peace and love.

LET IT BE

1John 1:9
If we confess our sins, He is faithful and just to forgive
us our sins and to cleanse from all unrighteousness.

O Lord let it be as it was in the Garden of Eden, a world of
peace and harmony.

Though we are not worthy, look upon us from above and
shower us with Thy love.

Be it tomorrow as it was today, a day of forgiving our sins and
allowing us to start anew.

Before the sun sets beyond yonder hill help us to forsake our
sinful ways and kneel before Thee in adoration.

As we forgive, so forgive us. As each day has a new beginning,
so may we.

Encourage the down trodden, touch the lives of the infirmed
heal the broken hearted and bring peace to all who seek Thee.

As we seek Thy will remove all doubt about thine abilities to
perform miracles in all aspects of our lives.

Let it be tomorrow as it was today, today being the first day of
the rest of our lives.

Thank you Lord for all that you have already done in our lives,
thank you for taking our place on the cross at Calvary.

LIKE IT IS

John 15:12-13
This is My commandment, that you love one another
as I have loved you. Greater love has no one than this,
than to lay down one's life for his friends.

Give I the love unto you that the Father has given unto me.

Let it be from this day forward a world full of love under the
control of the one who created you and me.

Let it be, let it be as it was before the Father gave it unto me.

Love conquers all and sets us free.

Love cannot be bound by the tethers of man, nor can it be
limited to just you and me.

The love of the Father flows like the endless river of time, it
prepares the heart to receive.

Nearer, nearer my heart grows to Thee, nearer my God to Thee.

The freer my soul, the closer to God I be.

Let it be as it was before the Father gave it unto me.

LIGHT OF THE WORLD

John 1:4-5
In Him was life, and the life was the light of men. And the light shines in the darkness, and the darkness did not comprehend it.

Jesus Christ is the "Light" of the world, and through Him all who live in this world can be saved.

He came to dispel the darkness and bring "Light" to the heart of all mankind.

Jesus being the Son of God (God on earth) brought hope for a lost people.

Those who listen and believe His teachings shall indeed be saved.

They shall dwell in His presence forever, knowing only peace, love, and joy, never again to be tempted by Satan.

Jesus came not into this world seeking wealth nor fame, He came to give to all who will listen and believe, eternal life.

Jesus showers us with gifts beyond price, gifts that cannot be bought with money, gifts that are free for the asking.

These gifts can turn a sinner into a saint, one who seeks to do the will of God in their lives.

The lost are too busy seeking the things that this world has to offer to serve God, their minds are clouded and they cannot see beyond their own self-centeredness

Things of this world stay in this world, even our fleshly bodies cannot leave this world, they shall return to the dust from which they were made.

Only the soul of man can live in both worlds, the flesh being corrupt must stay in this world, for in the spiritual world there is no corruption.

The spirit is subservient to God and if submissive to God while here on earth, it shall dwell with God throughout eternity.

Jesus came to be the "Light" of this world and the doorway to eternal life and only through Him can our souls enter the kingdom of God.

One day we shall shed our earthly form and return to our creator in our spiritual form to receive our just rewards. No one is exempt.

LIVE FOR JESUS

Philippians 1:21
For to me, to live is Christ, and to die is gain.

In this grave lies a child of God, one who found peace and love in His written word.

One who would rather die than live an unfruitful life for the Lord.

His numbered days he did pass searching the scriptures and praising God for all that, he had.

He no longer sails the vastness of the seas or climbs the highest mountains in search of treasures that can lead to an empty shell.

Instead, he now lives with our Creator in heaven above, enjoying the things He promises to those who live by His word.

The pleasures of the flesh he sought not and gained a crown when through the pearly gates he passed.

He found that the treasures of heaven far surpass the things he left behind, the things that rust and decay and only last for a day.

The treasures he found in the Lord's word carried him when through the valley of the shadow of sin he passed.

From his birth to the grave, he lived for Jesus and anchored himself in His word, never regretting giving up the treasures of earth for the pleasures of heaven.

LIVING WITH NATURE

Genesis 1:31
Then God saw everything that He had made, and indeed it was very good. So the evening and the morning were the sixth day.

God created the majestic mountains with cascading streams flowing towards the sea.

He created the waterfalls with rainbows forming in their mists as they plummet to the earth below.

The fish that inhabit the mountain streams are his creation too, along with the lofty trees that form the forest from sea to sea.

He made the bear that is king of his domain from the highest peaks to the green meadows far below.

On moon lit nights one can hear the wolf calling to its mate as his voice echoes from glen to glen.

Using hemlock and spruce bows for a bed, I sleep a peaceful sleep to the rising of the sun.

To see a deer and her fawn drinking from a mountain stream early in the morn warms the heart of a woodsman like me.

Spring, summer, winter or fall the great expanse of the mountain ranges is a beautiful place to be.

To commune with nature and all that God has made fills one with contentment and praise for the one and only God who created you and me.

The forest and mountains are not a place to tremble with fright, they are a place to relax and drink in the beauty that God created for the enjoyment of man.

When the snows begin to fly, do not run and hide, get out and snowshoe through the winter wonderland.

Trees laden with snow, their limbs touching the ground as if offering prayers before the throne of God is a beautiful sight to see.

They also offer shelter to the forest creatures and even man if he so decides.

The mountains and forest of this great land welcome all who are willing to leave civilization behind and live a simple life with God in mind.

There are no roads to follow, just pathways that lead to beauty sublime.

A campfire by night to keep warm, by day views that take your breath away.

The mountains offer a simple life, one free from the burdens of the city where steel and concrete prevail.

Every season has its own beauty, never two the same.

Living off the land is not as hard as it might seem, just a change in life style is all that is required of people like you and me.

The Indian tribes of the past wandered from place to place and lived in harmony with the creatures of the forest, taking only what they needed to survive.

We of today think of the Indian tribes of the past as being wild and of needing to be put away.

In reality, it is we who need to change our ways and live a life style free from the encumbrances of today, for instead of living with nature we fight her every step of the way.

LIKE UNTO A FOREST

Genesis 1:1
In the beginning God created the heavens and the earth.

A forest starts with just one small seed, driven by the wind until it finds its final resting place.

There it lies until the arrival of spring, when from within life stirs anew.

Its roots sink deep into the moisture laden soil, then inch by inch it extends itself heavenward.

As the years pass it grows to maturity, straight and tall it grows, some twenty, some thirty, some forty feet or more in height.

Its limbs offer shelter to the birds of the air; they raise their young along side of the squirrel and other tree lodging creatures created by God, From such a start a forest spreads across the land.

Just as a forest is started by a single seed, so was Christianity started by a single word.

In the beginning, God spoke and the universe leapt into existence, from that point God created one man (Adam) and from him mankind spread and grew to what mankind is today.

As there are many diverse trees in a forest so are there many diverse people in this world.

There is however a common thread between the spreading forest and mankind, that common thread being God, the one who created everything.

God so loved mankind that he sent his only Son, Jesus Christ, to reconcile mankind unto Himself.

Jesus came to pay the price for the sins of the whole world and that all who believe may have life eternal.

It is by choice that each individual comes to the cross and follows Jesus.

This is the path that God wants his children to walk, but to force them to do so would defeat the reason for creating mankind in the first place.

Through the Love of God all can triumph over sin, it is only when man falls to the temptations of sin that he becomes lost and comes in danger of the damnation.

God's plan for salvation becomes fruitful when man turns to Jesus Christ and accepts Him as their Savior, sent by God.

Jesus became the living word of God and from that word, Christianity has spread like the ever expanding forest that started from a single seed.

Jesus is the seed of Christianity and through Him, Christians will one day triumph over all adversity.

All else outside the protection and influence of God's love shall be cast into the lake of fire, including Satan and is fallen angels, never to tempt man again.

Like the forest that ever spreads, so shall the kingdom of God be, until one day everyone shall have heard the word of God, from one end of this world to the other.

LONG TIME AGO

John 8:36
Therefore if the Son makes you free, you shall be free
indeed.

Many, many long years ago love was released in this world
by the man who hung on the tree at Calvary.

His name was Jesus Christ and while on the cross, He negated
the power of Satan and set man free from the bondage of sin.

Those who believe are washed white as snow by the blood of
the Lamb.

Though Jesus was nailed hand and foot to that cross He never
lost His authority or dignity.

As his blood dripped to the ground, it spread the world around
and cleansed the repentant soul.

Even today in our modern times, the blood of the Lamb still
cleanses those who stand at the foot of the cross and accept Jesus as
the Lord of their lives.

Whether we are on top of the highest mountain or beneath the
depths of the sea, we are still under the influence of Jesus Christ,
for He is Lord of Lords and King of Kings no matter where we
might roam.

His love knows no bounds, nor is it out of the reach of whoever
may seek it in their lives.

Peace beyond understanding comes to those who put earthly
things aside and strife to live by Jesus' side.

You see, Jesus' love is for everyone, everywhere, worldwide,
from the planets in the heavens to the depths of the sea, Jesus is
there and is still alive.

It matters not in what time frame in history that we might live,
Jesus was there before we were and shall be there after we leave.

Jesus changes not from one generation to the next, he loves us all and only asks that we believe that He is who He claims to be and through such belief and faith in Him as being the creator of all, He would that all should spend eternity by His side.

What more will it take for us to come to our knees and proclaim Jesus Christ as Lord of all that we see?

LORD AND MASTER

Philippians 4:7
And the peace of God, which surpasses all
understanding, will guard your hearts and minds
through Christ Jesus.

In Christ's glory, let us stand and be judged by things of the
heart rather than the hand.

As the days, slip by one by one let Jesus' love in us shine.

Our eyes will behold His plan for man when heavenward we
gaze and come to understand.

When man's problems we come to face let us look heavenward
for the answers and glory in God's grace.

Peace can be ours at last when we turn our backs on the things
of the past and look to the future with hope and charity.

Serving God is far better than seeking earthly treasures, for
the things of God are eternal, while earthly treasures are like
quicksilver running through our hand.

In the heavens above rest our future, in the earth beneath rest
our past.

Heaven beholds the beautiful things of God, while the earth
swallows up the flesh without regard.

The heart and soul of man will never die, they will rest with
God if He so decides.

Our good deeds may be steppingstones to heaven, but without
Jesus Christ by our side, our future in heaven will be denied.

Peace, love, and joy, may they reign on earth and shape our
lives so that they may be more pleasing to God.

Behold, things of the past can keep us from reveling in God's
love, lest we look to the future with a new heart and the desire to
please God, with Him we can never reside.

Never again will we have to worry or be afraid, for God sent His Son, Jesus Christ, to take our place at Calvary.

It is with love that I write you these glad tidings and pray that you will accept Jesus Christ as the Son of God and Master of your life.

LOVE AND OBEY

1John 4:19, 21
We love Him because He first loved us.

If someone says, "I love God," and hates his brother, he is a liar, for he who does not love his brother whom he has seen, how can he love God whom he has not seen?

While on earth, our minds are clouded by the temptations of sin and we cannot see all that God has for those who love and obey.

We hope and pray for a bright tomorrow, but only God knows if we will enjoy the rest of today.

Plan for tomorrow, but live today as if you are going to meet Jesus face to face.

Fear not what might go wrong today, let not fear control what you will say or do today.

The length of life is not for us to know, we were created by God and to Him one day we must go.

Whether we live by the laws of God or live as if there will be no tomorrow is our choice and God will honor whatever way we choose to follow.

Though God does not honor those who go astray, He will not condemn them if they repent and return to the straight and narrow way.

Tomorrow may never come, so praise God for today and honor Him in all that you do and say.

Tonight before you go to sleep pray that God will keep you and guide you through the dark of the night and awaken you at the break of a new day.

A day that will bring you closer to your creator so that He can fulfill His will in your life and He will not have to say "I know thee not, go thy wicked way".

Repent and avoid the way of the wicked, for wide is the path that leads to destruction and narrow the way that leads to the preservation of the soul.

God loves those who will listen and obey, He also loves those who go astray, but will count them among the lost if they refuse to obey.

It is here and now that we must make our choices, for once death occurs it is too late to change our ways.

God awaits with open arms those who love and obey, He has a new home for all who bow before His throne and believe that Jesus is who He claims to be.

MAN'S LAST ACT

1Corinthians 15:52
In a moment, in the twinkling of an eye, at the last
trumpet. For the trumpet will sound, and the dead will
be raised incorruptible, and we shall be changed.

How often do we talk about death? Often we talk about eternal life with Jesus Christ and how wonderful it will be to be free from the sins of this world. Free from all disease, walking on the streets of pure gold.

But, in order to enjoy the fruits of eternal life and the freedoms that it will bring we first have to die. We have to lay down our physical life in order to enjoy eternal life.

I am here to tell you of an experience God allowed me to have just a short while ago.

One night while sleeping, I found myself on a journey of traveling through time and space.

I had no recollection of my past life; I had left everything and all memories of my physical life behind.

Once I started this journey there was no way of stopping it or changing its course. My spirit was on its way to reunite with its creator and from there to wherever it would be directed.

I recall having the sensation of traveling at a great speed in a darkened surrounding, not a black surrounding, just a darkened one.

In this darkened surrounding there were horizontal streaks of dim light. As though I was traveling through time and space so fast that the stars were nothing but streaks of dim light.

Whether this experience lasted just a few minutes or a longer period of time I do not know, for there was no sensation of time, just a sense of tremendous speed.

All during this experience of traveling through time and space I had the sense of perfect peace and no sense of fear or any hint of fear.

Before I reached my final destination I awoke from sleep and realized that this experience could not have been any more real than actually experiencing death and my spirit's final journey.

Three of the most impressive feeling I had during this period of time were, I carried none of my earthly experiences with me, the feeling of perfect peace, and the absence of all fear.

I would like to leave you with these verses from the King James version of the Bible. First Corinthians, 15: 54-55.

So when this corruptible shall have put on incorruption, and this mortal shall have put on immortality, then shall be brought to pass the saying that is written, Death is swallowed up in victory.

O death where is thy sting? O grave where is thy victory?

MAN'S STRUGGLE

John 3:3
Jesus answered and said unto him, "Most assuredly, I
say unto you, unless one is born again he cannot see the
kingdom of God."

We will never achieve perfection until we stand before Jesus
Christ Himself, for while living under the shadow of sin perfection
will never be ours.

In Romans, chapter three, verse twenty-three we read "For all
have sinned, and come short of the glory of God" (also read related
verses).

Sin and or the shadow of sin fogs the mind of man and he
cannot see perfection while under the influence of sin.

Whereas Adam and Eve lived in perfection before being
tempted by the serpent (Satan), but once they ate of the forbidden
fruit their eyes were opened and they perceived and lived in sin
from that moment on.

Since that time man has lived in a sin filled world and it has
been passed on from generation to generation ever since.

Sin itself has not changed from the day that man fell prey to sin,
although it may appear in a seemingly different form it is the same.

All sin is attributable to Satan and he is a liar and the father of
all lies.

It takes a lifetime of constant vigilance to protect ourselves
from sin and even then, we may unknowingly fall prey to sin.

As the Bible tells us to put on the full armor plate of God, so
must we do when sin tempts us.

Satan can only tempt us to sin; he cannot force us to sin. It is
we (you and I) who have the choice of accepting or rejecting those
temptations.

By using the armor plate of God, we can overcome Satan's assault against us.

The armor plate of God consists of the truths of God and our willingness to submit to those truths.

The truth being that God is supreme over everything, large or small and in Him is no evil, not even one iota.

God gave man free choice to do with his time here on earth as he pleases, and regardless of which way we choose to follow, God will honor it even though He may not condone our choices.

God put no boundaries on man's thoughts or activities.

We are in a spiritual battle, not a physical one, even though at times it may seem that way.

The flesh will never leave the realm of its earthly existence, but man's spirit will.

Man's spirit came from God and shall one-day return to God and upon its return God will judge us as to where we will spend eternity.

The repentant person that has accepted Jesus Christ as the Son of God shall dwell with God forever and ever. The unrepentant shall spend eternity separated from God forever and ever.

A lifetime of good deeds is not sufficient to get us into heaven; good deeds are the results of believing.

We will receive rewards for our good deeds when we enter heaven, but they are not a means by which we can get there.

There is only one way to enter heaven and that is to believe that Jesus Christ is the one and only Son of God and to put Him first in our lives.

In conclusion; following Jesus Christ and living by his commandments is the way of life for the believer and it takes a lifetime to prepare ourselves for the life that lies beyond the grave.

Also read John, chapter three.

No one can straighten out our life, but we ourselves. Others can encourage and help us see the truths that we should follow, but it is we who have to take God's truths into our heart and leave our old ways behind. In so doing we live a more Christ like life, which is the aim of all believers.

MEANT FOR GOOD

Romans 12:21
Do not be overcome by evil, but overcome evil
with good.

From the depths of despair I cry unto the Lord, "Why O
Lord do you not remove the pain of grief?"

The answer comes back, "It is for your own good that you
should suffer for your short comings."

"But Lord, I need your love, not your scorn."

All is silent from the Lord and I suffer for my own mistakes.

In the process of suffering, I unknowingly grow spiritually and
draw closer to God.

When the pain of grief is over, I am able to see that what I
thought was meant for evil was in reality meant for good.

Like the sunshine after the rain, God's loving care see me
through the trials that I need to bring me closer to Him.

Peace and love comes to those who use the armor plate of God
to repel the temptations of the flesh.

MY CONFESSION OF FAITH

Romans 10:10
For with the heart one believes unto righteousness, and
with the mouth confession is made unto salvation.

I believe that Jesus Christ is the one and only Son of God.

That God sent Jesus to be born of woman and to experience mortal life.

Among the things that Jesus accomplished while here on earth was the establishment of His Church.

Jesus defeated Satan while hanging on the cross of Calvary.

He gave us commandments to live by.

Proclaimed Himself as the doorway to heaven.

He gave Himself as an acceptable sacrifice for the sins of mankind.

He demonstrated God's love for all of mankind.

Jesus healed the sick.

Made the blind to see.

Made the lame to walk.

The miracles that he performed proved His power over earthly limitations.

Jesus demonstrated that death has no power over the body, by His own resurrection.

I am a witness of His love for all; He has healed me physically, and has turned a hardened sinner like myself into a saint.

He has granted me the gift of writing and has done so many things for me that I do not question His abilities or existence.

Jesus came to save all who will turn to Him and ask Him to come into their lives.

I believe that Jesus has the authority to forgive sin.

I believe that Jesus Christ was God incarnate here on earth.

I believe that Jesus has prepared a new world for those He has chosen to spend eternity with Him.

Jesus Christ is now and will forever be the Lord and Master of my life and I will endeavor to fulfill the tasks that He has asked of me and will in the future ask me to do, and I will do them to the best of my ability.

MINE EYES HAS SEEN THE GLORY OF THE LORD

Hebrews 12:7

If you endure chastening, God deals with you as with sons; for what son is there whom a father does not chasten?

Through His great love, God has healed my body and soul and has guided my feet in the way that I should go.

Some of my trials were hard to endure, but I clung to the promises of God and He saw me through.

From divorce to physical healing, I have through the grace of God prevailed and grown in His love.

For a time the sins that I indulged in gave me pleasure and I was blind to the truths that He later revealed to me.

God opened my eyes and I began to see that if I kept up my sinful ways that I would be lost forever, lost in the sea of sin.

He has spoken to me several times through the Holy Ghost and as a result, I have grown in His grace, learned to listen to that still small voice, the one that can be heard above all turmoil.

God has asked nothing in return for what He has given, He just gives and gives, and it is I who has changed, not He.

Through his gracious giving, I have learned to give without expecting something in return, and I give unto God all of the glory and honor that may in the future come to me.

I have learned to question not the ways of God, and give Him all credit lest I become puffed up and stand in the way of what He wants for me.

Regardless of my spiritual growth, I still remain a sinner and will remain so until the day I leave this world and join Him in heaven.

Until that time, I will endeavor to fulfill what He wants me to do and express His love in all that He wants me to do.

All is God's, I am just one of His children trying to spread His word through the pen and paper He put in my hands.

Sometimes I find it hard to fulfill my calling because of my weakness', I find it hard to let go of working full time and depend completely upon God to sustain me.

And yet I know that the day fast approaches when I will have to lay down the tools by which I now sustain myself.

Even though I look forward to that day I cannot help but think of how I will keep the wolf away from the door, and yet I know in my heart that God will supply all of my needs.

Looking back on my life I can see God's hand sustaining me, as He has guided and healed me in the past I know that He will continue to do the same as long as I live.

God has been and will continue to be the center of my life, for no one or anything can fill my life the way that He has.

My eyes has seen many things in this life, things that can only be explained as coming from God, not only to benefit myself, but all who I share them with, for surly I have seen the glory of God here on earth and I thank Him for such a privilege.

MY JESUS

Romans 10:9d
That if you confess with your mouth the Lord Jesus and believe in your heart that God raised Him from the dead, you will be saved.

Though the storms of life may rage, I will be safe in the arms of Jesus.

He will protect me whenever I call upon His name.

My fears will be belayed when His words I obey.

Jesus is the one who set me free when upon that cross at Calvary He gave His life so that I might live with Him one day.

Love is His motive, when He speaks I listen and change my ways.

Jesus will give me life eternal if I will but listen and obey.

Though He had no place to lay His head, the whole world is His.

Morning, noon, and night, if I walk the path He gave me to trod everything will be all right.

Jesus came into this world to right the wrongs and save us sinners from going to hell one day.

He opened the door to heaven for me and all who will listen and change their ways.

Jesus stood tall and strong and never wavered from doing His Father's will.

He set the wayward heart aglow and gave hope whenever He spoke.

Jesus is my Savior and in Him I have hope eternal.

Grace be unto all who seek to do His will.

While here, on earth, I will stand tall and proclaim His name and He in turn will declare me before His Father's throne.

I share with you my Jesus and pray that you will share Him with others as this pathway of life you trod.

MY PATHWAY

Psalm 23:3
He restores my soul; He leads me in the paths of
righteousness for his name sake.

Jesus is my pathway; He is my guide to heaven above.
He will comfort me if only I will listen to His voice as I cry out
in despair.

Amidst troubles and trials, He will guide my feet to the
pathway that He wants me to trod.

He will teach me if only I will listen and turn aside from the
sins that I try to hide.

O Lord I will follow wherever you guide me, I will not
question, nor will I hide from Thee.

During the dark of night or storm by day, I will follow if You
will be my guide.

When I see Thy light when I am in the darkness of sin I will
follow Thee all of the way to the foot of the cross.

Forgive me O Lord if I try to do things my way, for I am but a
lost sinner trying to find my way to Thy side.

Through the fog of sin I see dimly and am apt to go astray, but
if You will guide me I will follow Thee all of the way.

When at death's door I lie I pray that You will be by my side
and guide me all of the way.

Heaven will be my home if Thy light I follow when sin tries to
make me hide from Thee.

Peace will be mine if only I follow, follow Thee all of the way.

NEED YOU

Philippians 4:19
And my God shall provide all your need according to
His riches in glory by Christ Jesus.

Thank you God for sending your Son, Jesus Christ, to set us free so that we can follow you more closely.

Thank you for the Holy Spirit, the one who talks to us and guides us in our everyday living.

Thank you for being an inspiration to turn from sin and follow Thee.

Guide us as we come together as a congregation and form new committees for the advancement of our Church in and around the community.

As leader of one of these committees help me to know what is right to do and how to do it.

Being new to this kind of work direct me and open the doors that will lead to bringing the good news to those who need to hear it.

Without you O Lord, we can do nothing, but with You, all things are possible.

We must learn to walk before we can run, be gracious and show us the way to go.

By putting you first in our lives, we as a committee can do great things for the advancement of your kingdom here on earth.

May we be worthy of the calling that we have been appointed to do.

Bless us Lord Jesus as we go about your business, in Thy name we pray.

A-men

NEVER AGAIN

Matthew 5:21
You have heard that it was said to those of old, you shall not murder, and whoever murders will be in danger of the judgment.

Open my heart O Lord so that the floodgates of heaven can fill it with Your love.

Love for my sisters and brothers in Christ who come to Thee in search of what You have for those who follow You.

During the dark of night and the gloom of day let Your "Light" shine and release us from our sins I pray.

To you Lord God I commend my soul, restore it and return it to me so that I can live a life more pleasing to Thee.

Our little ones who have gone on before, due to losing their life at the hands of evil, I pray will await us as we pass through death's door.

It is with them in mind that I pray night and day that they will never have to suffer anymore at the hands of those lost in sin.

O Lord, change the mind of those who are about to commit murder, a sin of harming one of Your little ones.

Open their eyes so that they can see the folly of opposing Thee.

Instead may their hearts be filled with Thy love so that they can care in a loving way for the little ones who cannot defend themselves.

I pray that never again will a little one have fear for their lives while here on earth they abide.

NEVER CHANGING

Matthew 6:18
And I also say to you that you are Peter, and on this rock I will build My church, and the gates of Hades shall not prevail against it.

God loves His children one and all, he opens the door to heaven to all who believe.

By his word He protects those who turn to Him in their times of need.

He makes the rain to fall on all, great and small, the rich, the poor, and all in-between.

From birth to death, God guides and chastens all who choose to do His will.

Glory to God for the faithful who do not go astray and wait upon the Lord patiently.

From the rising of the sun to the setting of the moon God's word never changes, it remains the same.

When we put on the full armor plate of God, the evil one will never invade the soul of the saved.

Flesh and blood shall fade away, but the word of God shall stand forever and never change.

God holds the key to eternal life and He only gives it to those who believe.

Many shall come in the name of the Lord and proclaim that they are from God, but their lies shall be exposed and they shall surly die.

Upon God's request Jesus Christ came to earth and lived among His people and proclaimed the word of God, while here He established His Church that still remains.

Then as now, Jesus is its head and from this earth, it will never leave until Jesus returns to be its head priest, and then with Him, all believers will leave.

As the earth convulses and burns with fire many who were left will change their mind and bow before Jesus' throne and believe.

Those who refuse to bend their knees before Jesus' throne will mass together and try to destroy that which God proclaims.

Then with his mighty hand, God will rain down fire from heaven upon all who remain and sever the head of the serpent and cast them into the lake that burns with brimstone, there to remain for eternity.

Then shall peace and love reign throughout eternity, then shall all believers reign with Jesus Christ and live the life that God intended all of the time.

NEVER TOO LATE

2Peter 3:9
The Lord is not slack concerning His promise, as some count slackness, but is long suffering toward us, but not willing that any should perish but that all should come to repentance.

There was an old woman who lived by the side of the road. One day her husband suddenly died and she didn't know what she was going to do.

She cried and called out to God in anger and blamed Him for her husband's demise.

Slowly she withdrew and shut everyone out of her life, even her family too.

To make ends meet she took a job at the local bank where she worked until she retired. While there, she met a lot of people, but made no friends.

It was hard to know if she needed anything or became ill. Even when family called she never let them know how she really was.

She did have one friend that she looked after and confided in her only what she wanted her to know.

At times, she struggled with her health and went through an operation or two and only a few ever knew.

She was a good woman, yes indeed; she loved her grandchildren and never let them know the pain she carried day by day.

Though she had accepted Jesus Christ as her Lord and Savior earlier on in life, she turned from Him after her husband died.

Three years before her death she suffered a heart attack and this changed her life.

In her near death experience, she came to realize that she was wrong to shut out her family and friends and began to make amends.

She reached out to her sons and their families, and also to her brothers and sister. Old friendships were renewed and her life was once again fruitful.

During her final stay in the hospital just hours before she went into a coma she reaffirmed her belief in God and in his Son, Jesus Christ, through the encouragement of one of her sons.

She asked forgiveness of those whom she had offended and forgave those who had offended her. She could not rest until this was done. After this, she was at peace with herself and with God.

The old woman who lived by the side of the road passed quietly from this life to life eternal with her family by her side.

This is a story of how my sister lived and died. It is meant to show that no matter how life may treat you it is never too late to change or to make amends.

NEW BIRTH

Matthew 1:18
Now the birth of Jesus Christ was as follows; after His mother Mary was betrothed to Joseph, before they came together, she was found with child of the Holy Spirit.

Christmas is the season of new birth; we celebrate the birth of Jesus Christ by a virgin who never knew a man.

Although betrothed to Joseph, Mary was overshadowed by the Holy Spirit and conceived in her womb the Lord of the universe.

The one who spoke and the universe leapt into existence.

So great and Holy and yet humble enough to come to earth and live with created man.

Our Savior, Jesus Christ, was born into a sin-filled world and took our sins upon Himself and yet He remained sinless.

Tempted and taunted by Satan, Jesus withstood the pleasures of the flesh and won the hearts of all who believed.

Even from the womb, Jesus showed the power granted to Him from above, power to change lost sinners into saints.

His story has been told throughout the centuries and every time I hear it, my heart jumps for joy for He was the one who came to die for your sins and mine.

Not only for now, but also for all time to come Jesus Christ left us the greatest gift of all, a road map that can lead all sinners from the brink of hell to the serenity of paradise.

From His spoken word all of mankind, great and small can learn to live a life free from Satan's domain.

Triumphantly Jesus passed through this universe and so can we by following the example He set from His virgin birth.

Peace to all who come to the manger and worship the King of kings and Lord of lords, Jesus Christ the Son of God.

NEW WORLD

2corinthians 5:17
Therefore, if anyone is in Christ, he is a new creation; old tings have passed away; behold all things have become new.

There is a whole new world out there, one never seen by the eyes of man.

Sin so clouds the eyes of man that he cannot see beyond the sin that surrounds him.

Satan is the father of all sin and he will do all that he can to keep man from claiming his rightful place in God's plan for man.

There are temptations that many find tempting enough to indulge in without knowing that they face eternal separation from God for doing so.

Those caught in sin believe that they can change at anytime they want, but once enjoying the sins of the flesh, it is not as easy to give them up as one might think.

The more one gives in to the temptations of the flesh the further one gets from the salvation that is offered by God.

Like the clouds that obscure the sun, sin clouds our eyes and we lose sight of the way that God intended for us to follow.

An innocent gesture can turn out to be our downfall if we do not put it in its proper perspective.

The line between good intentions and a sinful act is very thin.

To break the chain of sin in many cases takes more effort than some are willing to give.

Our greatest tool against sin is prayer, prayer from the depths of our soul.

Along with prayer, we have to willingly turn complete control of our lives over to God, thus allowing His will to be done in our lives.

There is no sin that cannot be forgiven, no matter how egregious it might be.

In the eyes of God sin is sin, the only unforgivable sin there is, is blasphemy against the Holy Spirit.

A truly repentant heart, fervent prayer, and the desire to do God's will is the key to victory over the temptations of Satan.

Once faced with the truths of God, Satan is like a toothless tiger, all growl and no bite, this will cause him to flee from those who use the truths of God in their defense.

If one stands in the power of these truths, they are protected from Satan's onslaught.

Each and every day one has to renew their resolve as to who they want to follow, God or Satan and God will respect that decision.

Either decision produces consequences, to follow Satan will result in being cast into hell, to follow God will result in being allowed to enter heaven (new world) with all of its benefits and glory.

ONE BY ONE

Ecclesiastes 3:2
A time to be born, and a time to die; a time to plant, a
time to pluck what is planted.

One by one, we enter this world and one by one, we leave it, we are born alone and we die alone, even though we may be surrounded by friends and family.

One by one, we face the judgment seat of God and will hear him say "Welcome my child, you may enter heaven" or "I know thee not".

We ourselves are totally responsible for ourselves. Others may influence us, but we make the final decision as to whether to follow Jesus or to follow Satan.

Jesus is life eternal, following Satan leads to the second death (Separation from God for all of eternity).

Let not the pleasures of this life distract you on your journey to eternal life, for Satan will surly try to do so.

Lay aside those things that can blind you from the truths of God, take up your cross and follow Jesus and live.

It is Jesus who can set us free from the bondage of sin; it is His light that drives the darkness of sin away.

Jesus can be and will be with all who seek Him and He has provided a way to avoid being enslaved by sin from birth to death.

One by one, we journey the pathway of life and one by one, we either enter heaven or hell.

ONE DAY

John 7:6
Then Jesus said to them, "My time has not yet come, but your time is always ready."

This life is time to prepare ourselves for life beyond the grave.

The space and time that we now enjoy is but a snap of a finger compared to eternity.

From the cradle to the grave is but the wink of an eye in the scheme of things.

One day we will exchange this life for one that is not bound by any period of time, a place where there is no beginning and has no end.

There will be no sun, moon, stars, or darkness, just peace and love granted and sustained by God.

Jesus Christ shall be the "Light" thereof, and we like Him shall live in harmony for eternity, best of all there will be no sin or the slightest hint thereof.

While we yet live here on earth may we come to our senses and hold out our hand to our neighbor and explain one to the other that which we wish to understand.

Jesus Christ (The Son of God) came and lived among us to show us the way to live to obtain eternal life when we are lowered into our grave.

As Jesus was resurrected from the grave, so shall we rise in triumph over the sins that keep us from His side.

We, like Him, shall take on immortality on the other side of the grave, leaving our earthly sins behind.

One day when we leave this life behind, we will stand before our creator and receive that which we worked so hard for while on earth we did abide, whether it be for the good or the bad is not for us to decide.

Many shall be cast into hell because they never forgave or brought their frailties before the throne of God and let Him be the Master of their lives.

HIS CREATIVE HAND

Hebrews 1:10
And; You, Lord, in the beginning laid the foundation of
the earth, and the heavens are the work of your hands.

One day when this earth I leave I will ascend into the heavens and there I will travel throughout God's creation to see what I can see.

From star to star, I will wander, admiring their beauty.

I will observe the blue planet where I first believed, its beauty I will behold.

From galaxy to galaxy, I will roam and explore all that God lays before me, whatever it might be.

Each galaxy unique unto itself, created by the one who created all that I see.

Travel will be by the wink of an eye, nothing to close or too far away for one in a position such as I.

With an ever-expanding universe at my beck and call, but best of all, Jesus will be by my side.

Never again to face the trials of life on the earth that I left behind, just a bright and beautiful future where there is no time.

From one end of God's creation to the other I will roam and drink in the beauty that was there before man came on the scene.

No more sorrows, no more pain, just perfect health is all that will remain.

From the twinkling of distant stars to the glory of his throne, God is in everything I see.

One common thing will remain among those who chose to follow his ways, which is our dependence upon God, the one who created it all for those who believe.

One day all will prostate fall before His throne and praise His holy name.

OUR FUTURE

Revelation 21:7
He who overcomes shall inherit all things, and I will be
his God and he will be My son.

One day our bodies will return to the dust of the ground
from which they came.

They will no longer be full of life, and our minds will cease to
recall the pleasures that stirred within.

Our eyes will no longer behold the beauty displayed by God's
creative hand.

Our noses will no longer be tantalized by the fragrances that
brought our loved ones to mind, nor will they sense the salt in the
breezes that we once sailed by.

Our mouths will no longer taste the fruits that grew wild and
free, nor will our lips embrace our loved ones as they have done
before.

Our arms will only grasp the soil that we once tilled and life
came forth.

Nor will our feet run across the meadows and splash in the cold
ocean waves as they break upon the shore.

Our ears will be dull of hearing and will no longer hear the
songbirds call their mates as the warm spring weather encourages
life anew.

Oh, but our souls will begin life anew as we one by one we step
through the door of death and leave this world behind.

Our souls will race to be at our Creator's side, they will
embrace Him and praise His holy name.

Our feet will walk the streets of gold; our eyes will behold the
once unseen beauty that lies beyond the grave.

Our arms will embrace loved ones who went on before, and together we will sing praises to our one and only God.

Unable to please Him in the flesh, now we will see Him as He is and understand the mysteries that used to fog our minds.

Yes, we will run and not faint, we will behold beauty beyond what the flesh had in mind.

Death will no longer cause us fear, nor will we weep, for He will wipe all of our tears away and replace them with joy.

Our loving God has done and will continue to do all of these things, because He loves us and wants us to forever be a sheep of His pasture, protected by His almighty hand.

Yes, one day all of these things will come to pass, and what we leave behind will be a legacy as to how we lived before we stepped through the door of death and reaped our just rewards from the one who created us all, God.

THROUGH REPENTANCE

Proverbs 10:12
Hatred stirs up strife, but love covers all sins.

We often use words of love and adoration to try to drive sin from our door.

We engross ourselves in verses of scripture in our feeble efforts to keep from falling prey to the temptations of the flesh.

Just saying, "I will not listen to the voice of evil", is not enough to keep us from becoming embroiled in sin.

Only the truths of God as given in the pages of the Bible can keep us from being a disciple of Satan.

All of the good intentions in the world are worth nothing if the truths of God are ignored.

We are not strong enough or knowledgeable enough on our own to ward off the onslaught of Satan by ourselves.

Only the repentant heart, the one who allows God to have His way in their lives can be victorious over sin.

Satan (father of all sin) is a powerful adversary, but our triune God (Father, Son, and Holy Spirit) can prevail in our lives if we seek Him.

God will honor the decisions that we make for ourselves, whether they be for the good or the bad.

Man is in a sense the master of his own life, for God allows us to do with our lives whatever we choose.

When we commit sin, we know within ourselves that it is wrong, but we will often do it anyway, using one excuses or another to justify our actions.

Righteousness prevails when we put self, and self-interest aside and seek to do the will of God in our lives.

This God given life can be a great journey or it can be one of torment and frustration, we ourselves decide which it will be.

Regardless of how we behave, God shall prevail in the long run, for He is supreme over every aspect of our lives.

God wants nothing but good for all of us, but it is up to each individual as to how they conduct their lives, God will never force Himself or His love on anyone.

We (you and I) have the final say as to how we live our lives, God only judges us by the choices that we make.

Put God first, or Satan first is our choice to make, and by making no choice is putting Satan first.

Choose God and live, choose Satan and die the death of a self-convicted sinner.

We are all sinners, but a repentant sinner will be forgiven their sins, whereas a non-repentant sinner condemns himself or herself to hell, not God.

God loves all sinners, but will take only the repentant sinner unto Himself, which one are you?

JESUS IS THE ONLY WAY

John 14:6
Jesus said to him, "I am the way, the truth, and the life.
no one comes to the Father except through Me."

Open your heart and let Jesus' love enter therein.

It will cleanse your soul and set you free from the sins you now perceive.

There is no other way to enter heaven if you wish that to be your final goal.

For only through Jesus can we go to heaven when this world we leave.

Jesus gave his life as a sacrifice for your sins and mine when upon the cross He hung.

He opened the door and paved the way for sinners to repent so that to hell they will not go.

His love protects us as through this life we stroll, accept His love and live, reject it and spend eternity out in the cold.

Jesus suffered the consequences of your sins and mine; He brings comfort to the troubled soul.

Jesus left us a comforter when to His Father's side He arose, and promised to one-day return and claim His own.

Prepare yourself for this great and glorious day, when He comes, it would be nice to hear Him say, "Welcome my child. Come, spend eternity with Me."

OPEN YOUR HEART

Proverbs 18:24
A man who has friends must himself be friendly. But
there is a friend who sticks closer than a brother.

Let not the temptations of life distract you, keep your
thoughts on God and He will sustain you.

He will guide you as you go through life, keep not company
with those who do not listen to God.

Keep your heart open; close it not to that small still voice from
within that tries to keep you from going astray.

Rush not to judgment lest you come under the same
condemnation.

Be receptive to the word that can set you free.

Be a friend where a friend is needed.

Tell your story of how God has saved you from the jaws of
damnation, someone who needs to hear it may be listening.

Walk softly lest you stumble and fall into a pit of vipers.

Give as you were given, giving is more meaningful than
receiving.

Hold not back your testimony just because you think it
unworthy to be told.

Be bold in all that you do to promote the word of God and it
will not come back void.

God freely gives, not to just a selective few, but to all, great or
small.

As the rain falls on the just and unjust alike, so let your voice
be heard among all peoples.

Time is of the essence, for our days are numbered just as the
hairs of our head are numbered.

God was God yesterday, today, and tomorrow, He will be no different than He has always been.

God is a loving God and will share His kingdom with all who seek Him, no matter who they are or where they are from, all were created by God and are loved by Him equally.

OUR JOURNEY

Ecclesiastes 3:1
To everything there is a season, a time for every
purpose under heaven.

Our journey on this earth may be long or it may be short,
but regardless of its length, we are granted enough time to come to
Jesus Christ and know Him as our Lord and Savior.

Being young or old in no way affects our status as children of
God, for God loves and cares about all who traverse this life.

As we strive to comply with the way that God would have
us live we are at the same time preparing for our departure from
this life.

The more that we believe in the Son of God (Jesus Christ) the
more we detach ourselves from the desires of the flesh.

In leaving behind the desires of the flesh, we gain a greater
insight about the things of the spiritual realm.

All believers look forward to spending eternity with Jesus
Christ, but in order to enjoy this privilege we must lay this
life down.

Those we leave behind feel a great sense of loss and sometimes
lash out against God for taking our loved ones from us.

Eventually we come to understand that death is but the
doorway to a new and wonderful life with our creator, God.

A life free from the trials, diseases, and temptations of a
materialistic world, never more to shed tears of sorrow or worry
about loved ones during their times of peril.

Instead of grieving the loss of a loved one, we should celebrate
our loved ones triumph over this material life.

Celebrate that they now reside in heaven and are free from the
encumbrances of the flesh.

Shed tears of joy rather than tears of despair; sing praises unto Jesus Christ for coming to earth and revealing the pathway that leads to heaven's door.

Though our loved ones will be missed, know this; we too one day must pass through the door of death in order to receive our just rewards for following Jesus Christ while we were here on earth.

The journey of death is not to be feared, for from the moment that we close our eyes in death we open them to the beauty and splendor of heaven.

OUR OWN DESIRES

Galatians 5:1
Stand fast therefore in the liberty by which Christ has made us free, and do not be entangled again with a yoke of bondage.

In our older years, we are more receptive to sickness and disease that can cause us to fall into the slumber of death.

This life is but temporal and through the death of the flesh, God's kingdom is revealed unto us in all of its glory.

Things that we now cannot see will one day be a part of our lives.

We will dwell in the state of death until the resurrection of all flesh to a new life with God's Son, Jesus Christ.

The tares will have been separated from the wheat and the wheat gathered into Thy barns to live in love and peace forevermore.

As we live our lives here on earth so shall our future be when we close our eyes in death.

It is far better to forego the desires of the flesh and follow God through this life than it is to satisfy the desires of the flesh and spend eternity separated from Thee O God forever.

It is only through Thee that we can overcome the desires of the flesh and enter Thy kingdom when death relieves us of this life.

As we care for and love our neighbor here on earth, so shall we be loved and cared for when we close our eyes in death.

We cannot be malicious here on earth and expect love and forgiveness waiting for us on the other side of death's door.

Repent and forgive while there is still the breath of life in our bodies, for the day fast approaches when we will seal our own future within or outside of God's realm.

God has provided all of the tools that we need to live a righteous life, it is up to us to use these tools in order to avoid the consequences of a un-righteous life.

God would that no one be lost, He has granted us free choice to live or die according to our own desires.

OUR SOUL

Hebrews 10:39
But we are not of those who draw back to perdition,
but of those who believe in the saving of the soul.

God created us and within us, He placed our soul and set us free on the face of the earth to populate it as we would.

From mountain to mountain and shore to shore, we wandered and grew in the grace of God.

From this freedom came an obligation to live by the standards set forth by God, we commonly call them the Ten Commandments.

Many did and many still do live by the guide lines set forth by God, but a greater number prefer to live their lives to suit themselves.

They say that they love their neighbor, but their lifestyle and their actions say volumes as to how they really feel about their fellowman.

These are the ones who face a very uncertain future, for only the pure in heart shall inhabit the kingdom of God.

At the death of the body, the soul is set free from the confines of the body and will stand before the judgment seat of God to receive its just rewards.

It was intended for us to live a righteous life and by so doing avoid separation from God for eternity.

It is the soul that we should be concerned about while living in this sin filled world. The flesh shall perish until the final resurrection, when once again the soul and flesh shall reunite and spend eternity wherever God dictates.

Nothing of this world can leave this world; neither can the soul stay in this world upon the death of the flesh. It shall return unto the one who created it, God.

Take care and heed the word of God and dwell in peace and love forevermore.

OVERCOME

<hr>

John 16:33

"These things I have spoken to you, that in Me you may have peace. In the world you will have tribulation; but be of good cheer, I have overcome the world."

You and I are able to overcome our adversities in life because Jesus overcame the sins of the world on the cross at Calvary.

Through his crucifixion, burial and resurrection, Jesus proved that death can be overcome through faith in God.

Those who believe that Jesus Christ is who He claims to be shall be saved, those who do not believe face the second death (Separation from God for eternity).

Is it not better to err on the side of Jesus Christ than it is to disbelieve and face an uncertain destination after death?

God will honor whichever way we choose to believe and will reward us accordingly when we come before his judgment seat.

Rebuke the temptations of Satan and turn to God when in need and He will grant you protection under his sheltering wings.

It may seem easier to just go along with the temptations of Satan and to say to the hell with everything else, but this is just what Satan wants us to do.

In so doing we subject ourselves to the consequences of our sins and have only ourselves to blame when we walk through that door of death and have to make an accounting for our actions while here on earth.

It is a struggle from birth to death to avoid being lost due to the sins that face us every day of our lives.

But, the struggle to avoid being lost is well worth the effort when we look beyond ourselves and see the love and peace that can be ours when we follow Jesus Christ.

For Jesus Christ will reward those who stand guard at the gate of their minds and keep false doctrines from entering therein.

There are only two places to go after death, the just shall go to heaven and the unjust shall go to hell, the choice is ours.

To overcome sin is life; to succumb to sin is death.

THROUGH JESUS

1Corinthians 5:21
For He made Him who knew no sin to be sin for
us, that we might become the righteousness of God
in Him.

Jesus surly did come to save sinners from themselves, as sinners it is difficult to see our sins as clearly as someone else can.

Jesus saw sin for what it is, a way for Satan to separate us from the love of God, to be lost forever.

As throughout the ages, something or somebody has to be a sacrifice for our sins before we can become acceptable in the eyes of God.

Jesus Christ, (the only begotten Son of God), came and voluntarily became a sacrifice for our sins, and died on the cross at Calvary so that we (the children of God) could be free from the bondage of sin.

Jesus was not coerced in any way in accepting that position, He did it out of love for all of mankind.

Jesus was the only one who was strong enough to take on such a task and overcome the sins of this world without becoming a victim of sin.

Jesus was one hundred percent man, He was also one hundred percent God, and as such, He has the authority and power to grant eternal life to those who believe.

Jesus knew before He came to earth what He must do, and He carried out the will of God to the letter, and those who believe that Jesus Christ is the Son of God follow Him willingly and praise His Holy name with gladness.

Believing and knowing in their hearts that the only way to spend eternity with God is through His Son, Jesus Christ.

As Jesus overcame the sins of this world, so must we overcome the sins that besiege us, and we can only do this through Jesus Christ, not of ourselves, for we are not strong enough on our own to do so.

Be strong in the knowledge of Jesus Christ and fear not the evil that pervades this world, rather put your trust in Jesus Christ and rise above the temptations of Satan and live forever with Jesus Christ.

THE BEARER OF OUR SINS

Romans 5:19
For as by one man's disobedience many were made sinners, so also by one man's obedience many will be made righteous.

We come not to Christ to endure, but to overcome; it is only through Jesus Christ that we can overcome sin.

To just endure sin is not enough, sin must be overcome in order for us to advance in our quest to live a more Christ like life.

It is only through the submission to the will of the Lord that we are able to gather enough strength to overcome sin.

Sin is a very strong influence in our lives and we are not strong enough to overcome it by ourselves.

News stories of the day tell of people who commit crimes that they would not commit if they lived a Christ centered life.

Satan cares not whether we are rich or poor, common folks or famous, just as long as we turn from God and follow him.

This life is exactly what the Bible declares it to be, it is a spiritual battle between good and evil.

Evil rages all around us and there is only one-way not to become a victim of evil (Satan), and that is to put on the full armor plate of God, for where the "Light" and truths of God shines evil cannot exist.

Life is a constant struggle to avoid becoming a victim of evil, but the more we depend upon God the easier it is to overcome the sins that tempt us.

All are subjected to the temptations of sin, but the power and love of God will prevail if we choose to live life God's way.

It is our choice to either accept the temptations of sin or reject them; we are free moral agents, set free through the love of God to do as we please.

This life is where we make the decision as to where we will spend eternity, heaven or hell.

We do have the power to overcome sin through the sacrifice of Jesus Christ on the cross at Calvary.

PEACE AND UNDERSTANDING

Isaiah 26:3
You will keep him in perfect peace, whose mind is stayed on You, because he trusts in You.

Peace and understanding can come from tragedy through depending upon God to guide us back to solid ground.

Satan will do his best to distract us from the pathway that God has provided for those who choose to follow Him.

The only real tool that Satan has to distract us is temptation, as powerful a tool as it might be, he can in no wise force us to fall to his temptations against our will.

At the time, the temptation is very real and even overwhelming, but with determination and dependence upon God can keep one from falling prey to Satan's wishes.

These temptations and the urge to obey them may last for quite some time, but by using the truths of God that one knows at the time and standing fast in them can and will enable us to overcome the urge to obey Satan.

Even Christians are not immune to the temptations of Satan, knowledge of God and using that knowledge is the key to victory over the temptations of Satan.

In time, Satan will flee from the truths of God, for even he does not have the patience to out last the truths that are used against him.

Satan may be the prince of this world and may have authority to pursue his own agenda but his ability to force someone to follow his dictates is limited by God, as demonstrated in the book of Job.

The basic design of all difficult times that we face in life is for our advancement in the knowledge of God and our personal spiritual growth.

Those that God chastens will go through times of temptations and hardships to enhance their growth, but once through them they will be better equipped to fulfill God's will in their lives, whatever that might be.

As it has been said "Experience is the best teacher", and so it is, for God so loves us that He wants us to have these life experiences so that we will be better prepared to be able to reach out to our fellowman and help him through his trying times.

This in itself is demonstrating God's love and authority over all circumstances that we will be faced with as we make our journey through this life.

This life is a gift from God to do with as we feel is best for us, God allows us to make our own decisions and He also will judge us on the day of judgment by our decisions.

God has granted us free choice and He will respect our choices and allow us to follow them without interfering in the way that we conduct ourselves.

Peace and understanding does come from God through our obedience to His truths and living up to them to the best of our ability, and He will hold nothing back from those who love Him.

It may seem like a strange world that we live in, but every aspect of it is directly under the control of the one who created it, God.

God loves every person on the face of this planet, regardless of their background or behavior.

God has the ability to separate man from the evil that he partakes of, He loves the man and abhors the evil, and one day He will allow His Son, Jesus Christ, to return to earth and bring an end to all evil, including the father of all evil, Satan, then will peace and understanding reign forever.

PERFECTION

Romans 12:2
And do not be conformed to this world, but be transformed by the renewing of your mind, that you may prove what is that good and acceptable and perfect will of God.

In order for man to come to his full potential, he must first pass through the door of death and stand in the presence of God. There he will reflect the perfection of our Creator.

While in the flesh we are surrounded by the temptations of Satan and no matter how good we become we are unable to reach perfection.

The clouds of sin obscure our view and sin becomes a stumbling block, thus keeping us from what God intended.

Within every one is the perfection that God intended and as we pass beyond life this perfection will reveal itself.

Those left behind can see only one side of life and feel a great sense of loss when one of their loved ones passes on.

When we come to understand that death is just a stepping-stone to a new life without the harassment of sin then we are able to come to terms with our sense of loss and go on with our life.

It is God who holds the key to life and death and though we may not fully understand what life is all about we can trust that God is in full control and that He makes no mistakes.

God will never burden us with more than we can bear; this includes the loss of a loved one.

God will comfort us in our time of grief. Death is like a shadow of a cloud passing across the face of the earth.

When the cloud passes, the sun shines again and so it is with death, when it passes we find ourselves in the presence of God.

Death is for but a moment, life is eternal and when we pass from one to the other, we will enjoy that which God intended for us all along.

PERSONAL ENCOUNTER

2 Corinthians 5:10
For we all must appear before the judgment seat of
Christ, that each one may receive the things done in
the body, according to what he has done, whether good
or bad.

A personal encounter with Jesus Christ can and will change
one's life forever.

One can read the Bible and become knowledgeable about the
birth, life, death, and resurrection of our Lord and Savior, Jesus
Christ, and yet never have a personal relationship with Him.

A personal relationship with Jesus Christ changes one's
perspective about life here on earth and come to know that this life
is but one progressive step in the existence of man.

This life is either a time of growing closer to God or a time of
defeat by living a life of sin and crime under the influence of Satan.

Satan is a very real being and will if he can keep you from
ever becoming a disciple of Jesus Christ or having a meaningful
relationship with God.

A relationship with Jesus Christ negates all of Satan's influence
over our lives, for Jesus Christ is the Son of God and has absolute
power over everything, both material and spiritual.

All who fervently seek to have a personal relationship with
Jesus Christ will triumph over whatever sin Satan might entice
them with.

It is therefore imperative that one spends time seeking the grace
and forgiveness that Jesus Christ offers.

This grace and forgiveness will not come to you automatically,
we have to seek it with all of our heart and soul and make it a focal
point in our life.

If we slack off on our quest of having a personal relationship with Jesus Christ, we open ourselves up to the constant bombardment of temptations by Satan.

It is a constant struggle against the temptations of Satan from birth to death, but one that is worth whatever effort it will take to prevail against evil.

Once a close relationship with Jesus Christ is established Satan will seek ways to chip away at that relationship, for he is always a constant threat against any relationship with Jesus Christ.

Once a secure relationship is established with Jesus Christ it becomes easier to recognize Satan's threats and due battle against such intrusions.

One will be rewarded for fighting a good fight, perhaps not in this lifetime, but certainly in the life that lies beyond the grave.

It is better to sacrifice in this life and secure a place in God's kingdom beyond the grave than it is to have all that life before death has to offer.

The things of this life are temporal and the things of the life beyond the grave are forever.

In the end, it is we who makes the choices as to how we live our lives here on earth and it is we who will determine where we will spend eternity, God just honors our wishes.

Others will influence us as we travel through this life, some for the good, some for the bad, it is our decision as to who we allow to influence us, those who influence us for the good are of God, those for the bad are of Satan.

There are only two influences in this life, one is good (God), the other is bad (Satan) these two forces have always opposed each other, but in the end God shall prevail and his kingdom shall be established here on earth and Satan will never again have any influence over anything or anybody.

Glory, hallelujah, come Lord Jesus, come into my life today, so that I may claim for myself all that you have to offer, especially the offer to live with You throughout eternity.

POWER OF PRAYER

Romans 8:26
Likewise the spirit also helps in our weaknesses, for
we do not know what we should pray for as we ought,
but the Spirit Himself makes intercession for us with
groanings which cannot be uttered.

Prayer is the most powerful tool that a Christian or anyone
else could ever have in their pursuit of a healthy spiritual life.

Answered prayer can keep one alive longer than they would
without prayer.

As hard as it is to lose a loved one, perhaps it would be easier on
the dying if we prayed for a peaceful passing, instead of praying for
their recovery in a situation where death is inevitable.

Prolonging life can at times be more detrimental to the dying
rather than letting go and letting them return to God where you
know that there is perfect health, peace, and love awaiting them.

It is indeed a very hard and difficult decision to come to on the
part of the bereaving family and friends to pray for someone to be
relieved of their suffering through death.

This in no way means that anyone has the right to take a life or
even help someone end their life because of never ending pain and
suffering.

God is the giver of life and all life belongs to Him to control,
He has allotted so many days or years to all of us and we as
Christians respect His position and power.

To pray for God's will to be done in someone's life leaves
family and friends out of the business of asking God to prolong or
shorten life.

God so loves us that at times it seem as though He answers
prayer to heal and prolong life just to please us.

Where in some cases the sick and dying would suffer less if prayers were directed to helping someone die in peace, rather than live and suffer in agony.

God's mercy is unquestionable and is to be accepted without question, even in the case of the dying.

Death relieves bodily suffering, whereas praying for prolong life can produce more suffering rather than less.

When a loved one or friend dies it is we who are left behind who feel the sense of loss and we grieve because of the loss.

The departed is free from the pain and suffering and would not wish to return to our world of sin, for being with Jesus Christ is the goal of all believers.

Regardless of which side of prayer you fall on, prayer is still a very powerful tool and should be respected as a means of communicating with God, to make our wishes known to Him.

Without respect for God's will we are like dust in the wind, being blown hither and yon, never knowing where we will end up.

We are under God's control whether we like it or not, the sooner we come to Him and accept Him as Master of our lives the sooner we will find peace and accept His ways as a guide for our lives.

Whether we live long lives or short lives is not ours to know, what is ours is to conform to His ways and communicate with God through prayer

PRAISE GOD

Psalm 150:6
Let everything that has breath praise the Lord.

May the Lord your God watch over you while you sleep, may He awaken you refreshed at the dawn of a new day.

Praise Him morning, noon, and night, praise Him for all that He has done so that as sinners might begin life anew.

Bend to His will as you walk your pathway of life, listen for His calling and He will guide you through fair weather and foul.

His light will light your path and keep you from stumbling and falling prey to sin.

Peace will come when silent is your soul while waiting for God to answer your prayers.

Before the throne of God prostate fall, ask for His forgiveness for being among the greatest sinners of all.

Ask for forgiveness for cursing His name when things go awry, and the darkness of sin closes in.

Seek that love that can save sinners from eternal hell, for surly that is where all unrepentant souls shall dwell.

Proclaim the glory of God and stand for all of the world to see that sinners can change and live in harmony with their Creator.

Praise God wherever you are, and rise above your wicked ways and receive the greatest gift of all, eternal life with God.

PRAISE THE LORD

Revelation 19:5
Then a voice came from the throne saying, "Praise our God, all you His servants and those who fear Him, both small and great!"

I praise Thee almighty God for Thy mighty works here on earth and in the heavens above.

I praise Thee for the moon and stars by night and the warmth of the sun by day.

You sustain us and encourage us to go forward in search of Thy kingdom here on earth.

For the day fast approaches when there will no longer be a heaven or earth.

They shall pass away and those who repent not and reject Thy Son, Jesus Christ, shall be cast into outer darkness.

Comfort and heal us in our times of need, for only You can set us free from our infirmities.

Being the loving God that Thou art, You have provided us with a new heaven and a new earth, now unseen by the eyes of man.

It is with great anticipation that we look forward to the new life that You will have provided for those who believe.

Again, in this new life we will fall before Thy throne and praise Thee as we enjoy our new freedom from the oppressive ways of the old earth.

Blessed be Thy name now and forevermore. A-men

PRECIOUS FEW

1 Peter 2:9
But you are a chosen generation, a royal priesthood,
a holy nation, His own special people, that you may
proclaim the praises of Him who called you out of
darkness into His marvelous light.

Each and every one of us is unique, we are all different in
one way or the other and yet we are (or can be) one with God.

We are accosted every day by the temptations of the flesh,
orchestrated by Satan.

At times, we succumb to the temptations of Satan and lose
our way.

However, there is hope through Jesus Christ, for as we study
His word and contemplate His truths, one by one they awaken our
consciousness and become a light unto our path.

It isn't easy to let go of the pleasures of this world and allow the
truths of God to govern our lives.

It takes self-discipline and a fervent desire to live a more Christ
like life to overcome our earthly desires.

Within all of us is this desire, but it can be stifled by sin if we
allow sin to become foremost in our lives.

The road to eternal life is not an easy road to walk, for it is full
of the potholes of sin that can keep us from obtaining our goal.

The "Light" of God shines in all of our lives; it is we (you and
I) who must decide if we want to respond in a positive manner
towards that "Light".

It is there for all, but unfortunately, there are only a few who
respond in a positive way.

Too many go about claiming that they are a Christian, but
there are only a few who live, as a Christian should.

Unfortunately, the majority who choose to proclaim Jesus Christ as their Savior live lives that are contrary to His teachings. Many shall apply, but only a few shall be chosen.

Are you on your journey to eternal life or are you still distracted by the sins of the flesh?

We will never completely be free from the influence of sin, but we will come to the point where we will recognize sin for what it is and thus avoid it's full impact.

The rewards for following Jesus Christ will become apparent when we step through the door of death and come face to face with our Creator.

As different as we all might be it is possible for all of us to come together as one in Jesus Christ.

It is unfortunate that there will be only a precious few who will be chosen by God to spend eternity with Him. We all can be chosen if we choose to be.

HOLY GOD

1 Peter 1:16
Because it is written, be holy, for I am holy.

Oh precious God guide us as walk our pathway of life, keep us from the snare of the fowler.

Open our eyes so that we might see the beauty of Your creation and feel Thy great love that surrounds us.

Be as a beacon in the dark hours of our lives, until once again we walk in the sunshine of Your word.

Forgive us the sins that we commit day-by-day, help us turn our backs on the ways of the flesh, help us turn to you for guidance in all aspects of our lives.

Father, we come to Thee looking for a life, as You would have us to live.

We are sinners lost in the journey of life, not knowing right from wrong.

Thy mighty power of everlasting love can overcome the things of the flesh and set us free.

With your love comes forgiveness and the strength that we need to change our ways and live for You.

We humble ourselves before Thy throne and give thanks for all that You have done and will do in our lives.

We are not worthy to be one of your children; nevertheless, we praise You and seek to overcome whatever holds us from being close to You.

As we go about our daily lives we will keep You foremost in our thoughts and deeds.

We humble ourselves before Thy throne; with heads bowed, we ask these things in the name of Thy Son, Jesus Christ.

PROMISES

Hebrews 6:12
That you do not become sluggish, but imitate those who through faith and patience inherit the promises.

"Come to Me on bender knee, bow before My throne and I will grant thee thy fervent prayer."

"Like the days of old I will come and live with thee, My word will fill thy heart and through My Love you will overcome."

"Keep thine eye on Me, thy lips proclaiming My holy name."

"I will grant thee peace and you shall overcome thy greatest fears."

"I will not forsake thee nor leave you to face adversity alone."

"I will make the sun to warm thy face and the wind to always be gentle upon thy back."

"Come today; hesitate not lest you go astray, for the night can be long before the break of day."

"Evil lurks in the shadows, waiting to leap upon thee and keep thee from coming before My throne."

"Deny Satan through My word and hold My truths always before thee."

"My dear child I will never deny a willing heart who seeks to do My will."

"Now is the appointed hour, I will come again, this time I will not leave, I will live with thee forever."

Has He kept these promises in your life? He has in mine.

RAY OF HOPE

Psalm 71:5
For you are my hope, O Lord God; You are my trust
from my youth.

Bend thy knees before the throne of God and seek His grace.

Praise His name and proclaim Him as your friend and Lord of your life.

Bring to God your concerns and ask Him to intervene on your behalf.

Not that you may have your way, but that His will might be done in your life.

That your eyes might behold the might of His hand, and that you might feel His love from within.

O God, we cry unto Thee and ask forgiveness of our sinful ways.

We are weak O Lord, we can of ourselves do nothing, we are like the fleeting wind, not knowing where we will wander.

But You O Lord knoweth all things, we humble ourselves before Thee and ask that You guide our feet in the way that we should go.

Now and forevermore that You may be the guiding force in our lives, and that we might exemplify You in all that we do.

May peace and love prevail where now there is strife and discord.

We are blind and listening for Thy voice and will follow it all the days of our lives.

That we might dwell with Thee when this life we leave.

This is the prayer of sinners, trying to find their way.

REACH OUT

1 Timothy 4:14
Do not neglect the gift that is in you, which was given
to you by prophecy with the laying on of the hands of
the eldership.

Reach out to others right where you are, let not age or
circumstances keep you from being of service to God.

As time is ageless, so are the gifts that God bestows upon us.

God will reward those who heed His word and becomes a
friend to His neighbor.

Life experiences are to be shared, not stored in a vault to
gather dust.

There is someone who needs to hear your life experiences so
that they will not have to suffer as you have.

Open your heart to your calling, spread out the pages of your
life so that others may glean out truths that they need to improve
their lives and bring them closer to God.

As we grow in age we become history to the young and those
yet unborn, share your life experiences with them.

Through sharing, we are able to influence the future for the
better or the worse.

Where would we of today be if Jesus had not come to earth to
share His knowledge and wisdom with us?

We will never be as Jesus, but we can become more like Him
by honoring His teachings.

So can those who come after us benefit from that which we
leave behind.

There is no end as to how we can influence generations yet to
come, if only we use our God given gifts.

We are limited by our own self-imposed limits, for surly God never put any limits on our abilities.

Everyone has something to contribute to the advancement of God's kingdom here on earth, the timid soul may shy away from sharing their gifts, in so doing they inhibit their own spiritual growth.

We all need to be bold and share our God given gifts, for we never know when or how we can help our neighbor through a trying time.

Is it not time to step forward and share your gift with those you meet?

If nothing but a smile or a friendly greeting, it could and can change your own life and the way that you think about others.

Don't stifle that which was meant to benefit others, be a part in the uplifting of your fellowman when he is in need.

REACHING OUT

Isaiah 55:11
So shall My word be that goes forth from My mouth;
it shall not return to Me void, but it shall accomplish
what I please, and it shall prosper in the thing which I
sent it.

The more I try to control things the worse they get, because self gets in the way and hardens my heart to the word of God.

When finally I come to my senses, I begin to see where I went wrong.

When outside the will of God we are on our own and put life and limb in jeopardy.

Instead of listing for that small still voice, we invoke our own agenda and most of the time mess things up.

Instead of expounding the words of the Bible, we are inclined to keep them to ourselves.

It is our duty as a child of God to use what we have learned to the benefit of others.

By withholding, we not only rob our neighbor of what might help them, but also keep ourselves from growing in the word, as we should.

Reaching out to others enhances the growth of all concerned.

Peace comes to all who turn their lives over to God and allow Him to become the center of their lives.

The pathway of life is lined with the barbs of Satan that can keep us from the benefits that are ours just for the asking.

Even devoted Christians can be blinded by the pleasures of the flesh and lose their way.

Reaching out to others and seeking God's will can be a full time occupation, but at the same time be very rewarding.

In reaching out to others, God will reward those who put self second and Him first, to lose self in God will bring great rewards.

When we complain that our day is not going well, it may be that God has something better in store for us.

Like a flight that I recently took and was stranded in an airport for most of the day, discouraged and wondering if I would ever leave before the next day.

Then late that day the airline brought into service a much larger and luxurious plane to accommodate those who had been waiting.

It turned out that I met a person on that late flight that I was able to relate the word of God to; God's timing is always perfect.

To serve others and wait upon God is what we are called to do and in doing so we ourselves find peace amidst chaos.

REDEMPTION

PSALM 72:14
He will redeem their life from oppression and violence;
and precious shall be their blood in His sight.

The Lord God reached down with his mighty hand and lifted me out of the quicksand of sin and set me on solid ground.

He washed me with his shed blood and I became as clean as the new fallen snow.

Where once I was consumed by the pleasures of the flesh I now turn to God and receive heavenly rest.

Whereas Satan was once my next of kin, now Jesus is my mentor and has allowed the sunshine of His love to shine in my life.

It wasn't long ago that I frolicked in the land of sin, now my feet are headed homeward again.

The sun hardly shined in my life, now I cannot wait for a new day so that I can drink in the beauty of God's creation that surrounds me.

The stars at night have never been so bright as they are since the clouds of sin have passed me by.

I blamed all of my troubles on God and would not let Him in, now I open the door of peace and contentment wide and embrace God's love with a smile on my face.

From the path to hell to the gates of heaven, I have come and all it took was the fervent desire to rise above the sin that I was in.

God did all of the rest, in the twinkling of an eye He changed my life and made me a better person, one who looked up to heaven instead of looking down to hell.

Now I more fully understand what life is all about and why God sent his Son, Jesus Christ, to redeem sinners like me.

REMEMBER

Isaiah 9:6
Unto us a Child is born, unto us a Son is given; and the government shall be upon His shoulder. And His name shall be called Wonderful, Counselor, Mighty God, Everlasting Father, Prince of Peace.

Remember what the Christmas season is all about.

The coming of God to earth in the form of a baby by a virgin to save a remnant to glorify Himself.

Instead of Christmas gifts of material things that rust and decay, give of the heart and know that Jesus came to set you apart.

When sins abound and the temptations seem so right, remember that Baby Jesus came to share His love and set you right.

Through the darkness of long troublesome nights turn to Jesus and He will make everything aright.

Like the shepherds of old follow the star so bright and it will lead you to the crib of Innocence on a cold winter's night.

With Baby Jesus' smile of love, He can set you free from the bondage of hate and strife.

Fall before the cradle of love and Jesus will set you free from the bondage of sin and fill your heart with love for your fellowman and Him.

Through the tinsel and trappings of the season look for the gifts, that Jesus brought with Him.

The gifts of peace, love, compassion, forgiveness, freedom from the bondage of sin, and the promises of God, all lead to service to Jesus and your fellowman.

Young and old alike are all the same to Jesus, so at Christmas time hold hands with whomever you meet and share the gifts that Jesus brought that cold winter's night.

Jesus is the reason for the season and his gifts will bring peace and contentment to those who love Him and know that He is right.

REMEMBERING

Matthew 5:4
Blessed are those who mourn, for they shall be comforted.

Those who go before us are forerunners of our destiny.

As you mourn your loss, remember how your mother held you and coddled you when as a youngster you fell and scrapped your knees.

Encouraged you as you grew to your teenage years to live clean and cling to God's word when decisions you had to make.

When your skies were gray and the going hard, her council comforted you, and her loving hand kept you from going astray.

Remember the smile that greeted you when in her presence you walked and the scriptures she quoted by heart.

The stories that she relayed about relatives she knew before they went to their graves.

As the festive times of year rolled around, she opened her home and her heart to all who came through her door.

Then there were those times when she needed you to support her and how good it made you feel to help the one who had sacrificed so much for you.

The love of a daughter for her mother can best be expressed by being there when old age or sickness invades the life of the one who gave you birth.

As she enriched your life when you were young, so you enriched her life when she lay upon her bed as she embraced eternity.

Knowing in your heart that your mother now rejoices in the presence of God relieves some of the heartache of your loss.

As you can no longer embrace her bodily, remember that she is now being embraced by our Lord and Savior, Jesus Christ.

God must have a special place for mothers, both young and old alike, for they are God's way of spreading joy through the birth of their young.

God so loved mothers that He used a woman by which He sent His only Son, Jesus Christ into this world.

May God comfort you in your time of grieving, may He lay it on your heart that your beloved mother now resides in her rightful place, in the presence of Jesus Christ.

May He bring you peace and turn your sorrow to joy as you grieve the one you loved.

RENEWAL

2 Corinthians 4;16
Therefore we do not lose heart. Even though our outer man is perishing, yet the inward man is being renewed day by day.

Out of the depths of despair comes hope, hope of a new day, a day without the troubles that bind us.

When we step into the sunshine of the Lord we rejoice for the Lord can take our troubles away.

The Lord renews us day by day and showers us with his everlasting love and care.

When in prayer may Your voice be heard above the winds of sin?

May Your love calm the fears of the oppressed and bring peace to their troubled souls.

As the days and years pass, may Your encouragement and guiding hand open the doors that lead to peace and understanding.

Surly the sinful heart that terrorizes the innocent will one day be destroyed by their own hand.

For the consequences of sin is the death of the soul, separated from Thy righteousness by a great gulf that cannot be traversed.

As Your love is revealed to us may we not let an hour pass without praising You for all that you do for us day by day.

We give thanks almighty God for sending your Son, Jesus Christ, to live among us and showing us the way to eternal life.

It is with a humble heart and open mind that we kneel before Your throne and ask forgiveness for our sins.

Free us O Lord from the bondage that keeps us from enjoying the life that You intended for us to live.

It is through Thy Son, Jesus Christ that we ask that You fulfill our request so that we might live a life more pleasing to You.

We are sinners we know, but through submitting to Your word we can overcome and be renewed day by day and live a righteous life the rest of our days.

RESTORATION

Galatians 6:1
Brethren, if a man is overtaken in any trespass, you who are spiritual restore such a one in a spirit of gentleness, considering yourself lest you also be tempted.

Father God may your love touch the heart of those who try to manipulate and control the actions of Your Church.

May they come to know that the Church would prosper greatly without their manipulative ways.

Through prayer we the body of Your Church pray that the disobedient will come before Your throne and surrender to Your will.

That no one should be cast out through disobedience, but the Church would be better off without their controlling ways.

Father, we know that you love the person and despise the sin that tries to dictate and control what is not theirs to control.

We pray that the evil thoughts and deeds that keep our Church from growing be removed by our loving prayers.

We, the Church pray that the sin will be removed and be replaced with a loving, caring soul who will submit to your will.

It is hard to keep sin from penetrating the body of Christ, but when it does appear may Your love and our prayers overcome the sin in a loving way and restore harmony among Thy children.

We ask that You search our hearts and replace discord with love and the desire to do Your will, rather than ours.

May peace reign among all of Your Church and may it spread to the four corners of this world, and that this world may become as one with Thee, now and forevermore, Amen.

RESTORED

<hr/>

Psalm 23:3

He restores my soul; He leads me in the paths of righteousness for His name sake.

The Lord reached down with His mighty hand and saved an old sinner like me.

In the days of old I wandered around full of pride without shame, I worked hard and gained fortune and fame.

I partook of all that this world had to offer and stood high among my fellowmen.

I drove the finest cars and wore silk from the Orient; everything went according to my plan.

Other people looked up to me, how happy I was to explain how they too could enjoy the finest things in life like me.

I took things for granted, without thought of what I would do if suddenly I lost my health or a dollar or two.

God meant nothing to me, what would I want with him? I had all that this world had to offer, and I never saw my own sins.

Nothing or nobody could take away what I had, or so it occurred to me.

Then one-day things started to go wrong, my wife fell ill and was confined to her bed for a long, long time.

She kept trying to tell me that I should come to know the Lord, but my eyes and ears were closed, I was my own man and I needed no one to tell me what or what not to do.

Then the holdings upon which I had built my life began to disappear from view.

I would survive the loss, or so I thought, without help from anyone except me, myself, and I.

Within a year, I lost my wife along with everything else that I had held so dear.

What was a man like me to do? I was too proud to ask for help and too scared not to.

For months I lived hand to mouth and then the final blow, I suffered the loss of my health and knew not where to go.

All of my old friends were too busy to visit me or even ask if there was something that they could do.

Things went from bad to worse and one day I found myself living on the streets and eating in the soup kitchens that I once contributed to.

Then one wet stormy night I decided to end my life, my wife had died, my fortune had vanished from view, my health had failed, what else was I to do?

I was too proud to bend my knees before the throne of God; besides what could He do for someone like me?

I walked to the nearest bridge where the current ran strong, and was about to jump when I heard a voice saying to me, "Try just one more thing before you let go. Humble yourself before my throne and I will restore you and set you free."

I looked around and no man could I see, just the dark of the night with no one in sight.

Amazed and bewildered I stood there in the wet cold night and pondered in my heart what I had heard and what I should do.

Suddenly, like turning on a light I saw where I had gone wrong, then understanding and joy entered my soul.

I fell to my knees and whispered, "Was that you God I heard talking to me?"

From that moment on, I was free, free from the burdens that I had imposed upon myself while I was seeking fortune and fame.

I now stood like a man of God, one ready to face the rest of his life with Jesus by his side.

Soon my health returned and I was ready to retake my place in society, with humbleness in my heart, I joined the "Saints" of the Lord.

From that, time on God supplied all of my needs, my wants I left behind.

I now go about telling my story to all who will listen and encourage them to turn to God first in everything that they attempt to do.

Yes, God reached down with his mighty hand and saved an old sinner like me.

RESURRECTION DAY

John 11:25
Jesus said to her, "I am the resurrection and the life. He who believes in Me, though he may die, he shall live."

For now, some of the saints lay in the cold, cold, ground waiting for the resurrection day.

Glory, glory what a day that will be, Jesus will stand among the clouds for the whole world to see.

With a mighty shout, He will cause all the saints to rise from their graves, by His side they will stand.

All who know their shepherds voice will respond in a positive way, the rest will sleep on until the final judgment day.

Saints from around the world will walk hand in hand singing praises just as loud as they can.

Yes, that will be a glorious day in the life of man, for centuries it was foretold, now it is at hand, Jesus ruling over all of the earth and sea.

All who arise that day will spend eternity by Jesus' side, never again to be entangled in sin.

Peace will reign on earth for a thousand years, a peace not known since the fall of man.

Even the sea will give up her dead, for no matter where the saints might have laid their head the voice of Jesus will stir them to life.

Great will be the joy in the hearts of the saints, no one will be exempt from bowing their head.

This great day of days may be today or perhaps tomorrow, whether today or tomorrow, be ready my friend.

The clouds are gathering in the eastern sky, the earth is beginning to quake, soon the saints of the ages will stand at Jesus' feet.

ROLE MODEL

Mark 8:34
When He had called the people to Himself, with His disciples also, He said to them, "Whoever desire to come after Me, let him deny himself, and take up his cross and follow Me.

We as mortals are called to be role models to those who come after us.

We are to set an example for our children and grandchildren.

To stir within them the desire to seek God at an early age, to search out God's truths and to strive to incorporate them in their lives.

To live for God and imitate His love in our lives should be the desire of all.

In times of temptations reach out for the hand of God to hold and know that God will give us the strength to endure.

Open your heart and be receptive to that still small voice from within, for it is the voice of God speaking through the Holy Ghost answering your prayers.

The Holy Ghost does not repeat Himself; he makes Himself clear the first time.

It is with great joy that the receptive heart takes pleasure in fulfilling its calling and prostates fall before the throne of God in adoration.

Blessed be the one who forsakes the ways of the flesh and strives to leave a heritage worth more than a king's ransom.

A pathway worthy for generations to follow, for at its end is eternal life with God.

SEEKING

Luke 19:10
"For the Son of Man has come to seek and save that which was lost."

Like so many before me O Lord, I come to You seeking answers to life's problems.

Like; what am I supposed to do, how long before I meet you face to face, will I have enough to support myself and my family? Most of all, am I doing Thy will?

I come seeking answers, help me to be silent and listen for Your voice to guide me.

I would like to take life a little easier, I know that You told me that I would never have enough money to retire on and I accept that, but still I wonder what it would be like not to have to hold a steady job.

I don't want it to sound like I am complaining, for I am very grateful for still having good health and the ability to work.

I thank you Lord for all of the times You have spoken to me and guided me in the way that I should go.

Without your intervention in my life, I know that I would have passed from this life a long time ago.

I guess that I am like a lot of people, I want the best of both worlds and know that this cannot be so.

For either I follow You or follow the way of the flesh and I for one choose to follow you O Lord, come what may.

I thank you for being patient with one such as me, as I work my way through this life.

I know that one day I will be with You and be able to tell You face to face how grateful I am for having such a loving and caring God like You.

This world certainly would have a lot more chaos without Your loving care and guidance that You extend to those who seek You.

Again I thank you for all that You have done on my behalf and pray that more would follow You and come to the foot of Your cross where true compassion was shown to those who choose to follow You.

SERVING GOD

Galatians 5:13
For you, brethren, have been called to liberty; only do not use liberty as an opportunity for the flesh, but through love serve one another.

Glory be to God for righteousness sake, peace be to those who stand steadfast in His Love and in His word.

Now and forevermore may the will of God be made manifest in the lives of His children.

May the storms of life bring the sinner closer to God, and serve as an avenue of testimony.

Serving God satisfies the desire to be closer to God and wets the appetite of servitude.

Thanks and praises brings a smile to the face of the receiver and spurs him on to greater heights.

Now is the time to seek God, He waits for the submission of the rebellious soul.

The answers to all of life's problems can be found in the pages of the Holy Bible, the inspired word of God.

From Genesis to Revelation reflects the history of mankind, read it and find where you fit into the equation.

We all have our place in God's creation; will yours be with Jesus when this world you leave?

Our day of departure may be near, but the opportunity to spend eternity with Jesus Christ remains until we take our last breath here on earth.

SHARE

Hebrews 13:16
But do not forget to do good and to share, for with such sacrifices God is well pleased.

As you walk through the trials of this life fear them not for God will guide and comfort you.

When you go unto God with an open heart, He will fill it with peace and love.

Though the lessons of this life may seem harsh, it is because God loves you and through these lessons, you will grow in His sight.

As one grows in the knowledge of the Lord, they will be able to stand as a "Light" upon a hill and be an example of obedience to the Lord's calling.

Knowledge will enable you to go among the lost and preach the word of God and be a witness to His greatness.

Endure and be not slothful, bridle thy tongue and put forth thy right hand in peace and love and it shall return unto you a thousand fold.

Count not the ways of man and expect to live with the Lord forever, rather turn from your old ways and abide by the word of God and reap bountifully when you enter the gates of heaven.

When in the darkness of sin seek the Lord and He will free you from the bondage of sin, the Lord's "Light" shall shine upon you and comfort your soul.

Now is the time to seek the face of the Lord, hesitate not to take the first step, the Lord will open the door for you to step into his "Light".

A day without bondage to sin is worth more than all of the fine gold and jewels that man holds so dear.

Peace and love comes only from God and once obtained it cannot be hid under a bushel, it must be freely given to those in need.

You cannot bind God's love and save it for another day, for this will stifle it and render it as waste to be thrown away among the thorns.

You are unique and no one can take your place, you have much to offer. Share it with your brothers and sisters and it will not return unto you void.

SHARING

Acts 4:35
And they laid them at the apostles feet; and they distributed to each as anyone had need.

Share with others that which God has given to you so freely.

Whether it is wealth, special abilities, or knowledge, share it and in doing so, you are fulfilling God's plan for your life.

In the case of wealth, you cannot take even one red cent with you when you die, why not share your wealth with some deserving person or charity while you are still alive and can see the joy of that giving.

Sharing of knowledge advances someone else's ability to make a living.

In sharing, we are advancing God's kingdom here on earth. As a good idea can die on the vine, so can we if we horde our God given gifts and refuse to share them.

Wealth, knowledge, or any other God given gift was not meant to be hoarded, they were meant for the good of all.

Hoarding stagnates life and closes the door of opportunity for others.

Someone who hordes all that he receives is like the man in a small boat. One day he moved from one Island to another, so he loaded all of his possessions in a small boat and started to row to his new Island.

Along the way a tempest arose and the seas overwhelmed his small boat and it sank with all of his hoarded goods.

Had he shared his abundance with others before he moved he would not have lost it all in that storm and become penniless.

Therefore, it is with life, if we share our abundance with others we would not become burden down with them in fear of someone taking them from us.

Wealth can become as a millstone around our neck and we can drown in our own sea of unconcern for those around us.

The more we share the more God will bestow upon us, we cannot out give God.

God's wealth and knowledge is beyond our comprehension and He wants nothing more than to share it with us.

Bless and be blessed, hoard and die a pauper without friends.

Sharing is a gift from God, it is easy to give to those whom you love, it is divine to give to those whom you do not know, yet are in need.

SIMPLICITY

<hr>

Psalm 19:7
The law of the Lord is perfect, converting the soul; the testimony of the Lord is sure, making the wise simple.

The Bible is full of stories of people who God has used over the centuries to bring His word to all generations.

Over and over again God has used the simple people, ones with open minds and hearts to fulfill His will here on earth.

And so is the kingdom of God, its content and structure is based on the concept of simplicity, so simple that many there are who reject it on the grounds of simplicity.

They claim that something that simple cannot possibly be right; they believe that one must work in order to enjoy the life that comes after death.

From the beginning of the Bible to the end of the Bible, the things of God are gifts to mankind, gifts that need not be worked for, free for the acceptance.

Those who accept their gifts from God and act upon them know firsthand just how simple God has made it for them to carry out what they have been called upon to do.

No one has a legitimate excuse for refusing to fulfill their calling, because God will supply them with all that they need to fulfill that calling and will see to it that their gift will be used when and where He wants it used.

One may not live to see how their gift will be used or know how many lives it will touch, but one does not need to know such things, just that they have done what God has called them to do.

The things of God are so simple that many look right passed them and see them not and in so doing fall short of their potential, never having the satisfaction of leaving something for the next generation to contemplate.

That in itself is reward enough for the true believer, in fulfilling their calling they do it not for what they can get out of it, they do it out of hope that they can help someone else overcome their trials and tribulations in life.

Blessed be those who fulfill their calling, and more blessed yet are those who receive the benefit of someone else's gift and use it in their lives to advance the kingdom of God here on earth.

It is only through the love of God that any of us are willing to do whatever we can to help our neighbor.

No way can anyone pass through this life successfully without the guiding hand of God, and to know that through the simplicity of God's nature comes success.

Simplicity and success are synonymous and God has blessed us with both, then therefore it behooves us to open our hearts and accept that which will enable us to help our fellowman from generation to generation.

SOFT SPUN GOLD

Proverbs 25:10-11
Lest he who hears it expose your shame, and your reputation be ruined. A word fitly spoken is like apples of gold in settings of silver.

Once while traveling across this country so beautiful and wide I came across a town that lay in ruins by its greed for Soft Spun Gold (sinful pleasures of the flesh) and this is the story that I was told.

As I entered the town of Soft Spun Gold, I stopped for gas and inquired, "What kind of town is this town of Soft Spun Gold?"

The attendant replied, "My friend, it is a town where gold is spun so soft. A town where you can sell your soul for a pocket full of gold."

The attendant continued, "It all started when temptation turned this town into a town unashamed of sin for the gold that lies therein."

"At first it was just the gold that everyone was interested in, but as time passed this Soft Spun Gold clouded the minds of our virgins and old alike and they turned their heads from God."

Rambling on the attendant continued, "Soon it became common to trade gold for the pleasures of the flesh. It was no longer wrong to enjoy sex with strangers or for our young to have abortions when the occasion arose."

With tears in his eyes, "But lately it has gotten the attention of God and He has warned us to cease our sinful ways and the killing of the unborn. Cease or suffer the consequences as did Sodom and Gomorrah so many centuries ago."

Still with tears the attendant continued, "We tried, but Satan had turned our heads and we were weak, and just wanted to hide."

Now on his knees, "As you can see the flames of hell are consuming us one by one. Only this morning one of our most beloved citizens hung himself because of his shame. He had everything going for him until he tasted the fruit of sin. Just before he died he proclaimed that the fruit of sin was sweet in his mouth and yet bitter in his belly."

"Oh that we had listened to the prophets of old and turned from our evil ways, but it seems that the die has been cast and not one sinful soul in this town of Soft Spun Gold has mended their ways. You see, Satan promised to protect us even when we became old."

As the fires of hell, ravage this once proud and fruitful town the anguish cries of a once righteous people fills the ears of those who pass by and see the glow of destruction that shines in the sky.

Now regaining his feet the attendant continued, "Run my friend from this place of self destruction, before you too become entangled in the Soft Spun Gold that has lead us all to the brink of hell."

"God has turned His head from us and rightfully so, for sin will consume it's self and die the death of a wicked soul. Run, turn not back as Lot's wife did so long, long ago."

With hope in his voice the attendant urged, "Follow the straight and narrow that leads to the throne of God and thank Him for sending His Son, Jesus Christ, as a sacrifice for the sins of mankind. Hurry before you change your mind."

Now with sorrow in his voice, "I wish I had, but this Soft Spun Gold will not let me go and I shall suffer the death of the dammed as those did so long ago."

"Now hurry, go before you too trip and fall. What a shame that not even one precious child of God will be saved from this town where the Soft Spun Gold has clouded the minds of these once righteous souls."

With a trembling voice the attendant repeated, "Hurry, go while you still can, for once the Soft Spun Gold clouds your mind the devil owns your soul."

With haste, I paid for the gas and sped off, leaving dust behind. Headed back to the straight and narrow and praising God for the insight that He had just revealed to me as I stopped to refuel in the town of "Soft Spun Gold".

SOMETIMES

Psalm 23:4
Yea, though I walk through the valley of the shadow of death, I will feel no evil, for You are with me; Your rod and staff, they comfort me.

Dear God, sometimes You seem so far away, and sometimes I feel alone when I go to pray.

Sometimes I wonder if you even hear me when I say, "Father, help me this day to overcome the sin that stands in my way."

Sometimes I stumble and fall and wonder if life is worth it all.

Sometimes I wonder if You even love me as the Bible says, You don't seem to care what I say or do.

Sometimes when things go right, I thank You, but when I stray I often blame it on You.

These are the times I walk through the valley of shadows and the mountain peaks of sin tower high over me.

At these times peace is far from me, the shadow of gloom surrounds me.

In times like these, do You hear my cries of despair?

At the break of a new day when the clouds of sin have been blown away, it occurs to me that You did hear me and have answered my prayers.

It is then that I realize that it was I who turned from You, instead of You from me.

You send your tears in form of rain when sin I begin to obey.

At the break of day, You paint a beautiful sunrise to remind me that You love me and are trying to say, "Look at the picture I painted for you today."

It is then that I begin to climb out of the valley of despair and realize that only a loving Father like You would sacrifice His Son for a sinner such as me.

How could I have been such a fool to believe that You would leave me alone in this hostel world without Your Love to set me free.

Now instead of cursing you I bow my head before Your throne and praise You for all You have done for a sinner like me.

SPEAK TO ME

Matthew 10:20
For it is not you who speak, but the spirit of your
Father who speaks in you.

Create within me O Lord a pure heart, one that is open
to Thee.

One that will not question Thy ways, but accept every word
that comes from Your mouth as being a pearl of great price.

Words that will benefit my neighbor as well as myself, words
that will bring comfort to all who listen.

Grant me the courage to be bold when witnessing to those who
are lost, and stir life anew within the heart of the aged.

Speak to my heart O Lord; speak in a tongue that I can
understand, so that I might relay your message to my fellowman.

I pray that the rebellion within my mind will not keep me
from Your side, but rather, may your voice bring comfort to my
thirsty soul.

Bless and keep me from wandering into enemy territory where
the temptations of the flesh are strong, for I am weak and cannot
always tell the difference between right and wrong.

Speak to my soul O Lord; speak to me when I am faced with
decisions that will affect my future with Thee.

I search after Thy righteousness, may I drink of the wellspring
of Thy waters, waters that renews the desire for eternal live
with Thee.

In the dark of the night, speak to me O Lord; speak words that
I can use to encourage others to seek Thee before the break of day.

As the rising of the sun is to a new day, may Your words be
the beginning of life anew to all who seek to do Thy will, speak O
Lord, speak to those who search for Thee.

STAND WITH US

1 Corinthians 16:13
Watch, stand fast in the faith, be brave, be strong.

Bless us O Lord; bless us today as we pray for Your guidance that will keep us

As the sun and moon rise and fall, stand with us as the storms of life try to blow us away.

Guide our ship of life as we face the calamities of the day and bring us to a safe harbor where we will be safe from the wiles of Satan.

May we rest in Your loving arms as we recover from the sins that have lead us astray.

When we are upon the deep far from home, be our compass that will guide us to Thy side.

We will gladly step aside O Lord and let Thy will be fulfilled in our lives.

Be as a guiding "Light" set upon a hill O Lord, may Thy "Light" always shine in the darkness and drive all sin from our side.

Forgive us when we fail Thee O Lord forgive us we pray, stand with us night and day.

Thank you Lord for hearing and answering our prayers whether it be night or day.

Amen

SUBMISSION

James 4:7
Therefore submit to God. Resist the devil and he will
flee from you.

Unless our paths are made straight, we cannot serve God
with all of our heart and soul.

Sin can obscure our view and blind us to the truths that can set
us free; when we cling to sin, God we cannot see.

All sin is of Satan and when him we follow, we become
oblivious to the consequences of sin and think that we are doing
God's will.

To overcome sin, submit yourself to a higher power that power
comes from God; in His presence Satan's power is nullified.

Once our sins have been forgiven through repentance we are fit
to serve our Lord God in all that He asks us to do.

To humble ourselves before the throne of God and ask
forgiveness of our sins is an act of submission that can cleanse us of
all sin.

This cleansing clears our mind of sin and we become receptive
to God's calling and become capable of reaching out to others in
their times of need and be a living demonstration of the power of
God to change a sinner into a saint.

God made us all free agents and left to us as to whether we
want to live a godly life or a sin filled life.

In following God, we plant the seed of repentance, others may
water that seed and yet others may harvest, but whether we plant,
water, or harvest we are fulfilling the will of God.

Some will fall by the wayside and return to their sinful ways
and still believe that they are following what God wants them
to do.

We are our brother's keeper in the respect that it our responsibility to bring before our brother the word of God and witness to him what God has done in our lives.

The history of mankind has been written from beginning to end and presented to us through the inspired word of God in what we call the Holy Bible.

In knowing our beginning and our ending is surly, a compelling reason why we should be our brother's keeper and preach the word of God to all we meet.

Will you submit to the will of God and do your part in promoting the word of God right where you live or will or will you fall by the wayside and leave such things up to others?

SURRENDER

---

1 Corinthians 16:14
Let all you do be done in love.

Be unto the Lord as fertile ground, remove all evil from your thoughts and let your soul follow its Master, Jesus Christ.

Remove foul speech from your mouth and never again utter profanities against God or Jesus Christ.

Plow the furrows of your mind and water them with the truths as proclaimed by Jesus Christ.

Plant the seeds of Christianity in your heart and follow the path of righteousness.

Stand guard over what you allow to enter your mind, lest it becomes as the tares of the field.

Water your newly planted thoughts and allow them to come to fruition so that the harvest may be great.

As the potter shapes his vessels, so become in the hands of Jesus.

Surrender to Jesus Christ and become as a tool in His hands.

As a craftsman uses tools to fashion beauty from a piece of wood, so let Jesus fashion your life to display His love to those you meet.

Blessed is the man who forsakes the things of this world and becomes as a little child before the throne of the Lord.

Though the process be short or long do not forsake your journey for the short-term pleasures of the flesh.

Be diligent and stand steadfast in that which is good, it is best to lose a king's ransom than it is to lose one's soul.

Go thy way and be a "Light" unto the world, bring the "Light" of the Lord to all nations great and small.

TAKE JESUS DOWN
FROM THE CROSS

Galatians 6:14
But God forbid that I should boast except in the cross
of our Lord Jesus Christ, by whom the world has been
crucified to me, and I in the world.

Jesus hung on the cross at Calvary as a sacrifice for your sins
and mine; He now resides at His Father's side.

Jesus was obedient right up to the end, and so should we,
follow His example and spend eternity in Paradise.

Jesus walked this earth for just a short while, long enough to
stir the heart of all who come to believe.

He set a fire within the repentant soul, and gave hope to all, far
and wide.

He gave Himself to prove that this life is not all that there is, it
is but a stopover on the way to Paradise.

A place to learn and grow in grace, a place to come to know
that Jesus is the way, the truth, and the life, as He described.

Take Jesus down from the cross and invite Him into your
life, allow Him to be your Lord and guide as you make your way
through this sin-filled life.

He has treasures to give to you that cannot be bought or sold;
they are free to all who believe.

Among His gifts are; good health, peace of mind, freedom
from worry, freedom from want, most treasured is the gift of
fulfillment and love along with life eternal.

Jesus put Himself on the cross at Calvary for the sins of the
world so that you and I would not have to pay the price of our sins.
(If we repent of the same.)

Jesus freely gave His life for you and me, is it too much to ask to serve Him? I think not.

There are many ways to serve Jesus and they all lead to the foot of the cross, not to be nailed there, but to pay Jesus homage for what He did for every person ever born here on earth.

Again, take Jesus down from the cross and ask Him to come into your life, and to be what He came here to be, "The doorway to Paradise and eternal life."

TAKING THE STING
OUT OF LIFE

---

1 John 3:23
And this is His commandment; that we should believe
on the name of His Son Jesus Christ and love one
another, as He gave us commandment.

With the love that God expresses towards us how can we
go wrong?

If we go wrong, it is because we make the conscious decision to
go wrong, we chose to ignore what God has to offer.

Yes, God gave us freewill to live as we see fit for ourselves, but
He also holds us responsible for the way we live.

Accounting for the way that we live our lives is unavoidable,
after death, we will stand before the great Judgment Seat of God
and make an accounting of the way we lived our lives here on
earth.

God can and does bring our sins to mind when we least expect
it, this is to remind us that we are doing or about to do wrong and
gives us a chance to change our mind.

Many respect these reminders and change their decision to do
wrong and strive to live a better life, but the hard core sinners
turn their backs on God and continue to live in sin, thereby facing
separation from God forever.

The laws of God (the Ten Commandments) are for all to live
by, especially those who seek God and have the desire to live a life
more pleasing to Him.

The righteous want boundaries to live life by, therefore they
embrace the Ten Commandments with open arms.

No one is forced into following the ways of God, they do it because they want to, not because they have to.

God will chasten those who love Him for the purpose of making them better equipped to do His will while here on earth.

Putting God first takes the sting out of life and provides a place to go when life's problems seem to close in on us.

THANKS

Psalm 100:4
Enter into His gates with thanksgiving, and into His courts with praise. Be thankful to Him, and bless his name.

T— Think of God before you express yourself.
H— Have a nice day.
A— Ask God for forgiveness of your sins.
N— Never retire for the night with anger in your heart.
K— Know that you are a child of God and live accordingly.
S— Save time every day for prayer.

THE GREAT ARCHITECT

Luke 9:62
But Jesus said to him, "No one having put his hand to the plow, and looking back, is fit for the kingdom of God."

God is the architect who drew up and executed the plans for this great and wonderful planet that we live on.

It is but one small star among the numberless stars that make up our galaxy.

Here He deposited all of our needs for us to seek and explore.

We, you and I are the builders of God's kingdom here on earth.

If we do a shoddy job then His kingdom here on earth is weak and susceptible to infestation of evil.

On the other hand, if we are diligent and execute the plans according to how God drew them up then we will build a society that cannot be shaken when threatened by outside forces that are not of God.

When in the building if, we set back and let someone else do our part then we lose our rightful place in the new kingdom when it is finished.

God will only allow the willing and faithful workers here on earth to enter into the new kingdom when it is completed.

How else can it be, haven't we here on earth had enough of sin and discord, are not we ready for a time of pure bliss?

It is the faithful that goes beyond the call of duty and encourages the lost to change their ways, for they do not want to see anyone left behind when the last trumpet sounds.

God's plan is simple and easy to follow, it creates no burdens nor does it require us to do that which we are not capable of doing.

We do not have to give up self or our individuality to become a kingdom builder; rather it is because of our individuality that we are able to contribute to God's kingdom here on earth.

No two people have the exact same talent, we may do the same job, but in a different way.

Some can see the Master's plan and see the finished product where others see too much to be done and become overwhelmed and discouraged because of it.

No matter what your position is in the building of God's kingdom, do it according to your talent.

Everyone depends upon the other one to do their job as they are called to do it and to do it according to the Master's plan.

It is a consorted effort on the part of all involved to bring to a successful conclusion the tasks that lay ahead.

It is not a job that can be completed by any single generation; it is a job that requires many generations to complete.

When our tasks here on earth are completed, we will be ushered by angels into the presence of God.

There we will receive our just rewards for doing our part in the advancement of God's kingdom here on earth.

THE GREAT CONDUCTOR

Psalm 25:4-5
Show me Your ways. O Lord; teach me Your paths.
Lead me in Your truth and teach me, for You are the
God of my salvation; on You I will wait all day.

This life can be likened unto a scripted play, one that was scripted before the creation of day.

As a conductor directs his orchestra from the beginning to the end, so does God direct our lives if we live unto Him.

There are many variations to a piece of music just as there are many choices (variations) in this life.

As the music concludes with great fanfare, so do our lives when it is time for us to leave it behind.

God knows our every choice as we wander from sin to sin in search of peace and fulfillment.

There are those who rebel and become lost and God knew about them from the beginning of time.

God knows all things, for He wrote the script of life before time began and He set everything into motion.

He even made provisions for the sinner to turn from his wicked ways and seek His forgiveness.

We are all sinners and cannot see the overall picture; we just play out our part in the larger scheme of things.

If we knew all that God knows then we would be just like puppets on a string dancing to His tune.

This scenario would make for a very dull life, let alone one with no head nor tail.

God made no mistakes when He created man, it is man who tries to out guess God and do things his way.

Like a conductor corrects a musician when he plays the wrong note, so God lets us know when we are about to do something wrong.

We may not heed the advice of God and go ahead and commit the evil act, but in our heart we know that God was trying to keep us from harm.

It comes down to who we listen to and obey, the voice of God or the voice of Satan. We really do not have any excuse for committing sin.

As compelling, as Satan might be we have God to turn to and help us overcome the urge to do something wrong.

We of course make the final decision as to whom we obey in our daily lives.

God knows how weak we are and it gives Him great pleasure when we turn to Him to help us from doing wrong.

Our strength and help to resist evil comes from God and He will deny no one who turns to Him and asks for help.

Satan can be very persuasive, but he is no match for the greatest conductor of all time, God.

Leaning on the great conductor (God) makes great music, music that we can not only live with, but music that satisfies our soul and produces peace and harmony to all who hear and believe.

THOSE WHO DARE

James 1:5-6
If any of you lacks wisdom, let him ask God, who gives
to all liberally and without reproach and it will be given
to him. But let him ask in faith, with no doubting,
for he who doubts is like a wave of the sea driven and
tossed by the wind.

In every generation, there are those who dare to be different,
they ask the question, why?

Why does a certain thing do what it does, or why should I be
like others?

Then there are those who do not question the wisdom of the
past, they go on to search out the answers to man's problems.

These are the ones who step forth in faith and do what others
wish that they had the courage to do.

They look beyond themselves and venture into uncharted
waters, and at times sacrifice their lives so that others can have the
benefit of their endeavors.

Then there are those who just want to be different, break the
mold of tradition, move from place to place, helping those, they
meet, wherever they are.

To touch a life in a positive way is a gift from God, for there are
way too many who touch lives in negative ways, thereby creating
discord instead of promoting peace and harmony.

They use subtle ways to control others or to make them think
that they are doing good, when all along they have nothing but self-
interest in mind.

These are the ones with loud voices who stop at nothing to
get their way and when things go wrong they pass the blame on
someone else, rather than themselves.

Then there are those who are on the silent side and keep working for the benefit of all, they seek not self-satisfaction or want to be first to receive thanks for their efforts.

They do what they do out of love for their fellowman, and would prefer to remain in the background, rather than draw attention to themselves.

They would rather start some project and let someone else finish it and get all of the glory for a job well done.

They are sometimes referred to as the silent ones, ones who do something for the joy of doing it, rather than the glory.

The ones who work for glory often fall short of their intended goal, and then the silent ones step in and finish the project and without fanfare fade into the background.

Without these silent workers, many a project would never come to a successful conclusion, behind ever self-seeking executive there are the silent ones who seek nothing for themselves.

All generations have the self-seeking, self-serving, and glory-seeking people who have little regard for others, but thank God for the silent workers who want to see things completed to the benefit of all, rather than to benefit just a few.

These are the ones in the end who will be raised in glory, while the loud mouths of every generation are soon forgotten.

THREE CROSSES

2 Peter 3:9
The Lord is not slack concerning His promise, as some count slackness, but is long suffering towards us, not willing that any should perish but that all should come to repentance.

There were three crosses at Calvary the day that they crucified our Lord, Jesus.

The cross on the right and the one on the left were for two thieves that were deserving of death.

The one in the center was for our Lord and Master, Jesus Christ, the innocent Lamb of God, the one who paid the price for our sins.

On the cross to the left of Jesus was one who was convicted as a thief and never repented of his sins.

On the cross to the right of Jesus was also a thief convicted of his crimes and deserving of death.

But at the last moment of his life he repented of his sins and his soul was with Jesus in Paradise.

We of today are like those two thieves, we are also sinners deserving of death.

Some of us line up behind the thief that was crucified to the left of Jesus, (the unrepentant thief) and refuse to repent of our sins and accept Jesus Christ as the Son of God.

Some of us line up behind the thief that was crucified to the right of Jesus, (the repentant thief) and accept Jesus Christ as the Son of God.

Those of us today who refuse to accept Jesus as who He claims to be face eternity separated from God.

Those who stand with Jesus receive as their reward, eternal life and never have to face eternal death (separated from God for eternity).

It is here and now that we have to decide, as to whether we want to spend eternity with God or be separated from Him forever and ever.

Repent while there is still time, for the day fast approaches when it will be too late to change our minds, death will have overtaken us, at that point it is too late to choose.

Which line will you stand in, in your last days?

TIDBITS OF WISDOM

Proverbs 9:10
The fear of the Lord is the beginning of wisdom, and
the knowledge of the Holy One is understanding.

Blessed shall our nation be the day that we forsake our sins and
follow Thee.

Bible verse; Psalm 33:12

*   *   *

It is time to turn from our wicked ways and fly the banner of
freedom high.

Bible verse; Isaiah; 55:5-7

*   *   *

Knowing the way, the truth, and the life will never be until you
practice it in your own life.

Bible verse; John 14:6

*   *   *

It is God who works through you, not you who works
through God.

Bible verse; Ephesians 2:9-10

*   *   *

A proud and arrogant people shall be brought to their knees. A humble people shall be exalted and set free.

Bible verse; Proverbs; 16:5 James; 4:10

*   *   *

Hate begets hate and will result in the damnation of those who uphold hate and make excuses for it.

Bible verse; John; 15:22-23

*   *   *

Be not presumptuous enough to tell God what or what not to do and when to do it.

Bible verse; Psalms; 10:3-4

*   *   *

To love someone enough to let them go describes the kind of love God has for us.

Bible verse; Romans 5:8 John; 3:1

God forces no one to follow Him, we follow out of love.

Bible verse; John; 10:4

*   *   *

The open heart of innocence has compassion for all, regardless of their station in life.

Bible verse; Colossians 3:12-13

It matters not where or how we start life, what does matter is how we live our lives and how we end our lives, either for and with God or lost forever.

Bible verse; 1 Timothy 4:12 John 14:6

*   *   *

Come unto the Lord with an open heart and He will fulfill His will through you.

Bible verse; Deuteronomy 6:4-5 Philippians 2:13

*   *   *

A closed heart turneth the love of God away.

Bible verse; Hebrews 3:10-11

*   *   *

Be not found with thine eyes closed to the truths of God, for the day will come when you will be in need.

Bible verse; 2 Corinthians 13:6-8

*   *   *

A joyful heart is filled with love and compassion for his fellowman.

Bible verse; Psalms 51:10&13

*   *   *

Great is the love of God, greater yet is eternal life with God.

Bible verse; Psalms 33:5 1 John 5:11-13

*   *   *

Let your light shine so before your fellowman that they see God's influence in your life.

Bible verse; Matthew 5:14-16

*   *   *

Being handicapped is just another opportunity to exercise the love of God in your life and witness to others that handicaps can be overcome through divine intervention.

Bible verse; Matthew 11:4-5

*   *   *

You don't have to be honest, just clever, but remember that cleverness is an attribute of Satan.

Bible verse; Luke 16:11-13

We are a guest of God while living here on earth, therefore is it not proper to honor our host?

Bible verse; 1 Samuel 2:3

*   *   *

He who disgraces God will never sup with him, nor will he sleep in his tent.

Bible verse; Luke 14"24

As long as I walk with the Lord evil will never be my kin.

Bible verse; Joshua 22:5 1 John 1:6-7

*   *   *

God's "Light" shall shine upon the righteous and the un-righteous alike, but the un-righteous shall not comprehend it.

Bible verse; 2 Corinthians 4:3-4

*   *   *

It is now and ever shall be a day of growth for the righteous; the un-righteous shall thirst in the desert.

Bible verse; 2 Peter 3:17-18

*   *   *

Now is the time to display your love of the Lord, wait not for the sun to go down, for then no one can see it.

Bible verse; John 15:12

*   *   *

Is it not our duty to honor the Lord before His wrath falls upon our head?

Bible verse; Psalms 69:30 Romans 4:9

*   *   *

Obedience to the word of God displays our love for Him.

Bible verse; Romans 13:10

*   *   *

Those who search shall find, those who let others search for them shall be disappointed.

Bible verse; 1 Corinthians 2:10

*   *   *

It is little wonder we fail when we turn our backs and thoughts from God.

Bible verse; Jeremiah 3:21-22

God knows everyone on this earth by their first name and all lives are an open book to him.

Bible verse; Job 34:21-22 Matthew 6:4, 14

*   *   *

Lest we forget, God is God, creator of all.

Bible verse; Revelation 1:8, John 1:3, Colossians 1:16-19

*   *   *

Learn to trust in the midst of adversity.

Bible verse; 5:8-9

Turn to God when the dark clouds of sin begin to hem you in.

Bible verse; Matthew 1:21 1 Timothy 4:10

*   *   *

The Light of God nullifies the temptations of sin.

Bible verse; 1 John 1:5 John 8:12

*   *   *

The tides of life can carry us in many directions; the star of God (Jesus Christ) can lead us all to heaven.

Bible verse; Ezekiel 22:27 John 14:1-3

*   *   *

If heaven is where you want to be, then follow Jesus and you will be well pleased.

Bible verse; Matthew 16:24 2 Corinthians 4:8-9

*   *   *

God uses ordinary people to do extraordinary things.

Bible verse; 2 Timothy 2:21

*   *   *

Bless this new day O Lord; bless all it brings our way.

Bible verse; Ezekiel 34:26

*   *   *

He who has wisdom has the love of God in his heart.

Bible verse; Psalm 111:10

*　　*　　*

He that hateth his neighbor hateth God.

Bible verse; James 4:4

*　　*　　*

He who bends with the wind will never stand straight.

Bible verse; Nahum 1:3 James 1:6

A wicked man loveth iniquity, a righteous man honoreth God.

Bible verse; Isaiah 53:6 Psalms 69:30

*　　*　　*

Peace comes to those who seeketh God, The wicked dies by his own doing.

Bible verse; John 16:33 Isaiah 48:22

The Light of God cleanses the soul.

Bible verse; 2 Samuel 22:29

*　　*　　*

If you harbor resentment the Lord God will neither hear your prayers nor honor them, less it be a prayer for forgiveness.

Bible verse; Proverbs 13:15-17 2 Chronicles 30:27

TIME

Matthew 24:44
Therefore you also be ready for the Son of Man is
coming at an hour you do not expect.

Waste not thy time day or night, for once it is gone it can
never be retrieved.

Time wasted is like sleeping late in the morning and never
getting to see the picture that God paints every morning at the
rising of the sun.

God gave us time to be used wisely, not one second more or
one second less than is needed to fulfill His will in our lives.

Time is priceless and yet it cannot be bought or sold.

We had time yesterday, we have it now, but we are not
promised tomorrow, wasting time is frivolous, and an act of a
lost soul.

Time, like everything else in this world, one day it will run out
and there will be no more time.

Even time must stay in this world, for it too is tainted with sin
and purity only will be in heaven, and in eternity there is no time.

Time is either a friend or a foe, in youth time is a friend and it
seems endless, in old age time is a foe, as the end of this life is near.

We all have those days of being on time and days when there
doesn't seem to be enough time to get done all that we intended to
get done.

All of man's activities are measured in time, daylight and dark
are measured in time, we rush from place to place in given times,
and yet one-day time will be no more.

Time is a precious gift from God, He only created so much
time and like an hourglass the sands of time are running out.

Use wisely the time that you have left and follow the path in which God guides you, for one day there will be no tomorrow.

The greatest investment that one can make in the time that they have here on earth is to prepare themselves for where they want to spend eternity.

God has granted us enough time for that, waste it not and see your dreams of spending eternity with God fulfilled.

TO THE GLORY OF GOD

Luke 24:44

Then He said to them, "These are the words which I spoke to you while I was still with you, that all things must be fulfilled which were written in the Law of Moses and the Prophets and the Psalms concerning Me.

As a Christian, I pledge to uphold the high standards of Christian writing.

I pledge to promote the kingdom of God through my writings and put God first, self second.

I will not hold back any God inspired verse because I have not received any compensation from it.

The privilege of helping my fellowman through my writing will be reward enough.

If by the grace of God, I receive compensation for my effort I pledge to reach out to my fellow sojourners and help them along their way.

It was through God that I received the gift of writing and I give unto Him all of the recognition that I myself might receive.

God equipped me for writing through the trials that He allowed me to go through from my youth on up to the present time.

God has His ways of preparing one to carry out His will and I submit myself to whatever God has in store for me so that I might more fully be prepared to fulfill his will in my life.

When called to serve God I adjure you to follow your calling and do it to the glory of God, not self.

If monetary rewards come your way, do not let them overcome you and lose sight of what you were called to do.

Stand fast in your commitment to serve God regardless of whether you ever receive any compensation for your efforts or not.

For in honoring your commitment to God you are laying up treasures in heaven and you will be blessed many times over.

Not all are called to the same calling, but we all are called in one capacity or the other and it is our choice as to whether we honor our calling or not.

Not all will submit to their calling, but as for me, I do not want to have to stand before the judgment seat of God and try to explain why I did not answer my calling.

This should not be the only reason for answering ones calling, for the joy that comes with obeying God is far beyond any earthly reward.

In order for God's will to be done here on earth, it is up to the called to fulfill their calling and humbly bow before the throne of God and thank Him for choosing them to having His will fulfilled through them.

TOUCH OUR HEARTS

Colossians 3:15, 17
And let the peace of God rule in your hearts, to which also you were called in one body; and be thankful. And whatever you do in word or deed, do all in the name of the Lord Jesus, giving thanks to God the Father through Him.

Heavenly father we thank You for all that you provide.

At times, we do not appreciate half of what You provide and do, we take You for granted far too many times.

Even so, we thank You and ask You to touch our hearts and put them on fire for You.

Bless and heal the afflicted, but more importantly may Your will be done in our lives.

Touch the hearts of those who seek You, change their lives as You have changed mine.

Without you Lord God, we would all be lost, following false gods and condemned to hell when this earth we leave.

Father God, we thank You for your loving care and guidance, help us Father God from becoming prey to the evil one.

Only through You, can we overcome the sins of the flesh, for we are weak and easily lead astray.

Through you Almighty God, we can overcome all adversities.

Guide us Lord God to touch other lives and share with others that which You have given unto us.

Thank you for reminding me to pray, "What can I do to serve You while I remain here on earth?" instead of asking You to do something for me.

TOUCH US

John 16:33
"These things I have spoken to you, that in Me you may have peace. In the world you will have tribulation; but be of good cheer, I have overcome the world."

Gracious God, touch the heart of the unrepentant soul.

Instill in them the desire to seek You, lest they be lost forever.

That their thoughts might dwell on You, rather than on the sins that binds them.

Through You almighty God we can be set free from the bondage of sin.

You provide a safe haven for all who stand up to Satan and declare, "No, I do not want to indulge in any activity that will endanger my relationship with God."

With this declaration, Satan will seek others to deceive who do not have such a firm relationship with God.

We thank you loving Father for having a positive effect on the lives of all believers.

Grant us peace, strengthen us, and protect us as we walk the pathway of life.

Thank You for sending Your Son, Jesus Christ, as a sacrifice for our sins, for without His sacrifice we would face a very bleak future.

We praise You and ask these things in the name of Thy Son, Jesus Christ.

WHAT WILL YOU LEAVE?

Matthew 6:19-21

"Do not lay up for yourselves treasures on earth, where moth and rust destroy and where thieves break in and steal; but lay up for yourselves treasures in heaven, where neither moth nor rust destroys and where thieves do not beak in and steal. For where your treasure is, there your heart will be also."

What have you to leave the next generation? Have you worked hard and filled your warehouses with gold, silver, and material things?

Will your offspring's lives be enriched by what you will leave behind?

The wealth of the world will make your children's lives easier and enable them to live a life with a sense of financial security, but what about their spiritual life?

Have you told them of how God has blessed you in your life, or how He has healed you without medical assistance?

Which would you rather received from your parents, a financial windfall or a promise that God will supply all of your needs, including good health?

I for one can claim that God has supplied all of my needs, including the ability to earn enough money to pay my own way through this life.

God has for years healed my body and given me good health and I know that He will continue to do so for the rest of my life.

God made it known to me that I would not have enough money to retire on, in saying so He assured me that I would never go without.

A rich spiritual heritage is worth much more than any material inheritance. Spiritual gifts are for a lifetime, material wealth can erode away for no apparent reason, leaving one destitute and comfortless.

God will comfort those who seek His face and will supply them with the means by which they can supply their own needs.

By cultivating a good spiritual life, one will know how to guide the next generation in the path in which they should walk.

There are many poor who are richer than those who lay up earthly treasures for themselves and those who come after them.

God does not reward according to the pocketbook, He rewards according to what is in their heart.

Just as it is easier for a camel to go through the eye of a needle than a rich man to enter the kingdom of God, neither can anyone with an evil intent in their heart enter heaven.

Evil intent can be hidden from his fellowman, but God sees in secret places and judges on things hidden in the recesses of our heart.

Lest we forget, God knows us better than we know ourselves.

It is with great pride that we leave our offspring with the good things of life, but is it not more satisfying to leave a rich spiritual inheritance, rather than a material one.

Material things will rust and decay, while spiritual things will endure throughout eternity.

WHERE DO YOU STAND?

Deuteronomy 6:13
You shall fear the Lord your God and serve Him, and shall take oaths in His name.

Are you a product of society, conformed to the ways of man?

Do you hesitate to expound the words of God when someone is in need?

Does the thought of being associated with a church make you reconsider joining?

Do you make excuses for not accepting an invitation to attend a church function?

Do you attend church only when it is convenient for you?

Do you hesitate to join a church because you think that you will be put on a committee and have to help run church affairs?

Do you hold back your support to a church just because you do not like the way that some of the members conduct themselves?

Do you hold back from serving on committees because you think you are too busy?

Do you refuse to serve as a chairman of a committee because you think that you might be criticized?

When was the last time you took time to pray and humble yourself before God?

What if, just what if God had not come to earth through Jesus Christ and gave his life as a sacrifice for your sins and mine?

Where would you or I spend eternity if Jesus Christ had not returned to heaven to prepare a place for us?

Is it not our responsibility to respond to the word of God so that the door to hell is not opened to us?

This in itself should be enough for us to pursue the road laid out by Jesus Christ and claim our rightful place in the kingdom of God.

What are you waiting for?

Open your heart to God, accept His Son, Jesus Christ as your Lord and Savior, seek out a church where the word of God is preached and practiced.

Join that church and commit yourself to serving on committees, reach out to those in need, you have more to give than you think you have.

All too soon, it will be too late to do what you should have been doing all along.

THERE IS A PRICE TO BE PAID FOR DISOBEDIENCE

Psalm 9:16-17
The Lord is known by the judgment He executes; the wicked is snared in the work of his own hand. The wicked shall be turned into hell, and all the nations who forget God.

Kings and nobles of the past, allowed riches, power, and position to motivate them more that the love of God.

As consequences for allowing, the riches of this world to distract them many died with no dignity.

Much is the same today, the ones who allow wealth, power, and station in live blind them to the need of the downtrodden face the same demise.

It is far better to be rich in the knowledge of God than it is to own all of the gold that there is in the world.

Monetary wealth can only supply the wants of humanity; it cannot buy a place in the heavenly realm.

The poor with the desire to fulfill the will of God in their lives are far richer than those who seek only the glory and prestige that gold and wealth can bring.

God filled this world with precious stones and gold and silver that was intended to be used to benefit all people, but a greedy few try to hoard this bonanza of wealth for their own personal gain.

From God's point of view, with wealth comes the responsibility of caring for the down trodden of this world, but few there be who apply this philosophy to their lives.

Those who share their prosperity with the needy are laying up treasures in heaven that will serve them well when they leave this world.

Those who fill their storehouses with wealth for their old age are turning their backs on God and are full of fear that they will not have enough to last them while in this world.

Man has to make a choice to serve God or obey the whispers of Satan who tempts him to hoard wealth without regard for his fellowman.

Rich or poor is not the question, the question is what is in your heart, the desire to help your fellowman or has greed turned you from your responsibility.

WITH GOD

Psalm 46:10
Be still and know that I am God; I will be exalted among the nations, I will be exalted in the earth!

It is with God that my soul shall dwell, my flesh shall return to the dust of the ground from which it came.

In the twinkling of an eye, I shall be changed, from death to life eternal I shall rise.

The grace of God abounds and comforts my soul, in righteousness I shall walk all of my days.

As long as I live by God's commands, my life will be one of peace and harmony.

My problems will melt away if I turn them over to God and stand out of the way.

It is in obedience that God expects me to stand, when I refuse He just steps aside and lets me have my way.

Like a loving father He waits for me to return, seeking His forgiveness for my sins of the day.

If it is with God, I wish to be, I will come to Him in humility and seek His face before in death I dwell.

Once death has overtaken me it will be too late to change my ways, I must do it while I still have a breath to breathe.

From birth to death, I belong to God, but it is I who has to reconcile myself to live the life that God intended if I wish to live with Him on the other side.

GUIDE AND DIRECT

1Thessalonians 5:17, 18, 21, 22
Pray without ceasing, in everything give thanks; for this is the will of God in Christ Jesus for you. Test all things; hold fast to what is good. Abstain from every form of evil.

Precious Jesus, guide the hands of the surgeon as he closes the wounds of the afflicted.

Soften the heart of the politician to enact laws equal for all.

The hand of the tradesman as they build and rebuild our places of abode.

Guide the hand of the poet and writer as they convey your words and works to the whole world.

May the choirs sing songs of adoration as they come before Thy throne in humbleness of heart.

Touch the heart of those who choose not to accept Thy Son, Jesus Christ, so that they too might find peace through knowing the One who created them.

Encourage all who You have granted special gifts, that they might be bold so that your love might be spread throughout the world.

We look forward to the day when Jesus returns to this world, so that there will be no more pain or strife, just peace and harmony among all people.

We thank Thee O Lord God for this world that You have provided for us and for loving us enough to provide a way that we (your children) might live with Thee for eternity.

All of these requests we bring before Thee in the name of Thy Son, Jesus Christ, A-men.

List of books
by Merrill Phillips

MY CALLING
TELL ME AGAIN GRAMPA
PRICE OF FREEDOM
LIVING BY HIS WORD
THOUGHTS FOR THE SOUL
POTOPURRI
FOOD FOR THOUGHT
WALKING THE PATHWAY OF LIFE
LIGHTING OUR WAY
WHERE THE SAND MEETS THE SEA

The author was born and raised in Chatham, Mass. and has lived in many different parts of this great country. He now resides in the small town of Barton, Ms. where he spends his days putting his writings into book form. He hopes this devotional will help inspire people to turn to God in their times of need and come know His Son, Jesus Christ as their Lord and Savior.